Curry Culture

A Very British Love Affair

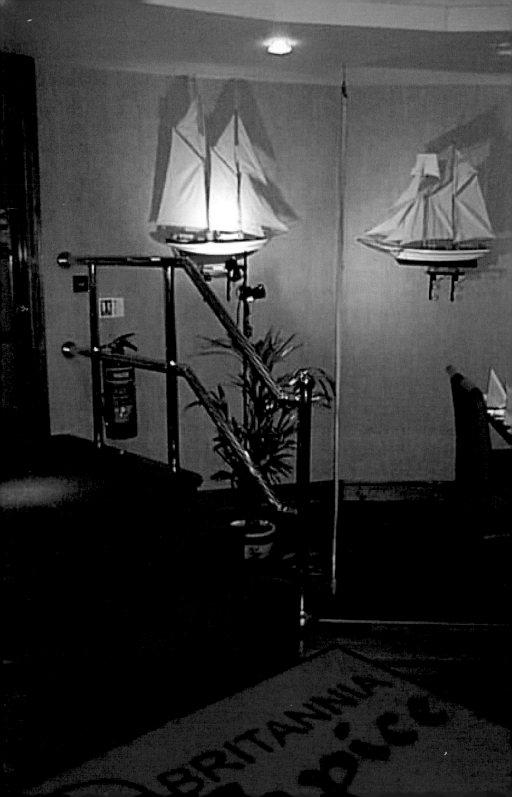

Curry Culture

Peter & Colleen Grove

MENU Magazine
Ethnic food & drink news linking dine out with dine in

Husband-and-wife team Peter and Colleen Grove are leading experts in the history of ethnic food, and Indian food in particular. They are regular contributors to radio and TV and are authors of *The Real Curry Restaurant Guide; Curry, Spice and All Things Nice*, and several other restaurant guides and have been editors of *Menu Magazine* for over seven years.

In 1994 at the request of leading Indian restaurants they set up the *National Dome Grading Scheme* and have operated a *Best in Britain Awards(BIBA)* scheme to highlight excellence in the industry for the past thirteen years.

Their two websites, *www.menumagazine.co.uk* and *www.menu2menu.com* receive a fantastic combined total of almost 1 million hits worldwide a month.

First published in 2005 by Menu Publications Ltd.
PO Box 416, Surbiton, Surrey, KT1 9BJ, United Kingdom
T : 020 8397 7517 F : 020 8397 4593 : email : groveint@aol.com

© Menu Publications Ltd./Text © Peter & Colleen Grove
ISBN : 0-9548303-0-X   £11.99

Printed & bound by Premier Print Group, Bow, London E1.

Contents

Page			Features
8	Chapter 1	Origins	
			20 Portuguese in India
			29 First Man of Curry
34	Chapter 2	One on Every High Street	
			58 The Ubiquitius Tandoor
			62 What is a Balti?
74	Chapter 3	On or Off the Bone, Sir?	
			86 Chicken Tikka Masala
			104 Chilli
114	Chapter 4	Behind the Beaded Curtain	
			124 The Wahhab Way
			140 Cyrus Todiwala MBE
154	Chapter 5	Curry on Eating	
			178 Critics
			184 Charity
194	Chapter 6	Epilogue	
210		Glossary	
212		Bibliography	
214		Index	

foreword

As someone who has experienced at first hand the 'curry' restaurant industry develop from its traditional base in Britain to recognition as a top international cuisine, I feel privileged to be asked to offer a few words by way of introduction to what I am sure will be the definitive work on the history of Indian food and restaurants in Britain. I have known the authors for many years but am still astounded at the wealth of information they have managed to produce in this work.

I had no real experience of Indian food (apart from being Indian) until 1992 and even after a few boom years there were no restaurants really aiming at Michelin recognition. Now as General Manager of Tamarind I am proud to represent one of the only two Indian restaurants in Britain to presently hold a Michelin star but I feel we do so as representatives of the entire industry (ed's note - Tamarind became the only Indian restaurant to hold a Michelin star in 2005).

In Britain, fans of Indian food can now choose from the most basic but still highly popular curry house to up-market establishments that compete favourably with the top restaurants in any other cuisine sector. No cuisine stands still, which is what makes Indian cuisine so exciting.

We still have a wealth of traditional dishes almost unknown outside their local regions in the subcontinent and yet we have exciting chefs who are pushing out the taste boundaries so the cuisine has a long way to go.

The 'Indian' restaurant in Britain has a proud heritage and one that has made it part of the fabric of the British way of life. The story is one of hard work, commitment and more than a little humour and I commend this work to the reader as a celebration of all that has been achieved in our industry thus far.

Rajesh Suri - General Manager,
Tamarind Restaurant, Mayfair, London W1

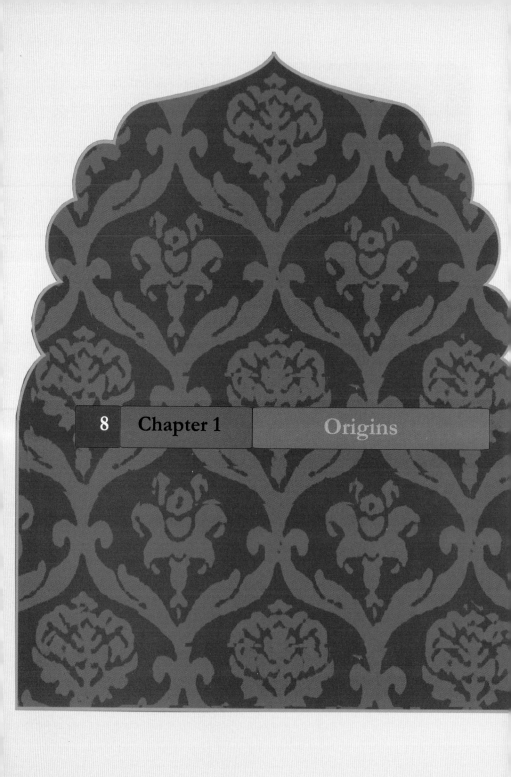

Chapter 1

Origins

love it or loathe it, you just can't ignore it. It sparks passion in some, poems in others. It has been talked about in glowing terms by government ministers and flown halfway around the world to pamper pining film stars.

It is very much part of British culture today but its roots reach back across the centuries.

What is it about curry that turns the British on? After, all it's just a spicy stew, isn't it? And why is it just the British? It hasn't caught on in the same way at all with the French, Germans, Italians or Americans! Even in India, the Indian restaurant hasn't really taken off - most people prefer Chinese when they eat out.

Boom time

Take Chicken Tikka Masala, for example: Marks & Spencer claim to sell 18 tonnes a week; 23 million portions a year are sold in Indian restaurants; 10 tonnes of it a day are produced by Noon Products, who produce chilled products for Sainsbury's and Waitrose, amongst others; Most of the schools and charities in Sylhet, Bangladesh are run by proceeds from the sales of 'CTM' in Britain.

Even in India, the Indian restaurant hasn't really taken off - most people prefer Chinese when they eat out.

There are Chicken Tikka Masala sandwiches, wraps, pizzas, crisps and even lasagne, and if these don't fill the gap, there are over 8,500 Bangladeshi, Indian, Pakistani and Nepalese restaurants where you can find many versions of it. To cap it all, Chef Iftekar Haris from Newport, Gwent has even written a musical in praise of it!

In March 2001, the highest Cook in the land at the time, Foreign Minister Robin Cook, that is, declared proudly that, "Chicken Tikka Masala is now Britain's true national dish...". Whether he was hoping for a discount at his local curry house or merely playing to a multi-cultural crowd is not clear, but there is no doubting the impact the 'curry' phenomenon has had on Britain and the British way of life.

You can tell we love curry, as with every other British icon, we make a joke out of it. In the mid-1970's when the number of high street curry houses was spiralling, there was the one about the ideal girlfriend - waist-height

with a flat head to put your lager on, who then turns into a curry after the pubs close.

But is it just a modern thing? Is it even only a 'lad' thing? Did its popularity really only grow because the curry house was the only licensed place left open after the pubs closed? Or does it go back further than that?

Well, indeed, it does go back further than that, a lot further in fact. Way back to the Stone Age, when our distant ancestors were chewing horseradish seeds to spice up their food.

Origins of the word

The word 'curry' itself has also been around a bit longer than most people think. Most pundits have settled on the origins being the Tamil word *kari* meaning spiced sauce. In his excellent *Oxford Companion to Food*, Alan Davidson quotes this as a fact and supports it with reference to the accounts from a Dutch traveller in 1598 referring to a dish called *Carriel*, (but note, not curry). He also refers to a Portuguese cookery book from the seventeenth century called *Arte do Cozinha*, with a chilli-based recipe called *caril*, (once again, not the word curry).

In her book, *50 Great Curries of India*, Camellia Panjabi says the word today simply means 'gravy'. She also credits the Tamil word *kaari or kaaree* as the origin, but with some reservations, noting that in the north of India, where the English first landed in 1608 then subsequently in 1612, a gravy dish is called *khadi*.

Pat Chapman of The Curry Club, (founded in the early 1980's to bring all curry lovers together), offers several possibilities:- *karahi or karai* (Hindi) from the wok-shaped cooking dish, *kari* from the Tamil or *Turkuri* a seasonal sauce or stew.

The one thing all these experts seem to agree on is that the word originates from India and was adapted and adopted, initially by the Portuguese, and then by the British Raj. There are, however, some interesting historical footnotes which may require us to think again.

In fact, the history of the spicy stew goes way back to the dawn of time. Archaeologists have found clay tablets in Mesopotamia (now Iraq), written in the cuneform text of the Sumerians, an ancient advanced civilisation in the region, which details a recipe for a meat dish to be eaten with a spicy sauce and bread. Dating back to 1,700 B.C., the tablets also say that it is an offering dedicated to the gods, possibly Marduk, the most powerful deity of the time. Could this have been the first recorded curry?

The British people have long been fond of a bit of spice. We've already mentioned horseradish, the fiery root of which has been an indispensable partner to that other British love, Roast beef. But, even as far back as the Roman occupation, we were starting to enjoy the new commodities that arrived with them.

A big breakthrough came in AD40 , when a Greek named Hippolas discovered that the monsoon winds cut the voyage time to the land of spice considerably. Like a lot of Greeks of the time, he worked for the Roman Empire, which was keen to exploit this new theory. Shortly afterwards, the Romans had broken the Arab trade monopoly, bringing pepper from India and cinnamon from Ceylon (Sri Lanka).

A big breakthrough came in Ad40, when a Greek named Hippolas discovered that the monsoon winds cut the voyage time to the land of spice considerably.

The real key to the spread of spices, however, remained the Arab trader. In spite of this early setback to their total dominance in spice trading, the

Caravanserai, (Arab spice traders) managed to keep their hold over the rest of the trade for centuries.

In AD711 the Moors took over *Al Andalus* (Southern Spain), and brought cinnamon, nutmeg, pepper, aniseed, sesame, cumin, coriander, ginger and caraway with them. These new spices spread throughout Europe and in AD982 in England, King Aethelred II levied a special Christmas and Easter tax, payable in pepper, on German ships coming up the Thames to trade at London Bridge.

Ginger reached Britain by the tenth century after gaining great popularity in Germany a century before. The special crocuses from which saffron is obtained started to be grown in Saffron Walden in Essex (hence the name), whilst elsewhere in Europe, caraway was to be found growing naturally and was already in widespread use.

Meanwhile, back on the Indian subcontinent, in AD630 the new religion of Islam appeared, and by AD712, the Muslims invaded *Sind* (Pakistan) bringing their influence to bear on India and its cuisine.

Another great influence on Indian cuisine was the arrival of a boatload of Parsees from Persia. Ironically, fleeing the persecution of Islam in AD745, they landed at Gujarat in north-western India and were allowed to settle there, adding a new dimension to the local food with the addition of dried fruits such as apricot.

East and West

Eleventh century Europe saw the focus shift to the invasion of England by the Normans, introducing new elements to a culture initially influenced by the Romans but which was now largely isolated.

The coming of William the Conqueror in 1066 had been a real watershed in English cuisine. He used dining as an entertainment designed to appeal to people from all walks of life by introducing three new major feast days: Christmas was celebrated at Gloucester with people of all stations invited; Easter at Winchester; Whitsun at Westminster. The influence of the

Normans also saw a break from the influence of the Scandinavian Norsemen in British cuisine. The real revolution, however, came in the time of Richard I, the Lionheart.

The first Crusade was mounted in 1095 and, although the stay-away monarch who spoke no English had no personal effect on cuisine, the comings and goings of so many important Europeans throughout the Middle East did.

The last Crusade to set out from Europe was declared in 1270 by Louis of France, but he reached no further than Tunisia before inconveniently dying, ending a period that was highly significant in introducing many foods and cooking styles from the East to Western kitchens.

The influence from France and from the returning Crusaders ensured a wide range of herbs and spices were added to those of Roman Britain and used in noble kitchens. Basil, borage, mallow, dittany, true love, fennel, ginger, cardamom, galingale, (a more peppery type of ginger), clove, sorrel, mustard seed, nutmeg, anise, mace, mint, peppercorns and cinnamon were all in use in Mediaeval times. Salt, whose Roman name for its provision was synonymous with income (hence *sal*ary), was considered so important it was stored in a special vault in the Tower of London. The result was a highly spiced cuisine for the nobility.

The use of spice in food denoted wealth and power, with cinnamon being the most popular.

However, this craze for all things spicy didn't spread across all classes. Frumenty was one of the staple dishes for the masses - wheat berries, long boiled in broth or milk, flavoured with available local herbs, or sweetened with honey, to make it more interesting.

The use of spices from the East had become a status symbol by 1200, and the more exotic and flavoured a feast was, the more the host was admired and envied. The European preoccupation with spice was born - and not simply because they were useful for disguising the taste of rotting meat, either.

In Mediaeval times dinner guests would select their food from 'chargers'  full of food, which was then placed on large slices of bread, or 'trenchers', which were used as edible plates and were often coloured and flavoured with parsley or saffron. The hearty soul who could eat all his food and finish off the trencher too was known as a trencherman, a term still in use today. Menus were large and extensive, but small portions were deemed correct and tasting more important than gorging. Because the only shopping lists that survive from the period are for huge state banquets, the Mediaeval noble class has developed a bit of reputation for excess. However, it must be remembered that these were big events, with the general public invited to watch on, with some lucky few managing to obtain a small taste of the spread..

The use of spice in food denoted wealth and power, with cinnamon being the most popular, having been in use in wine from Anglo-Saxon times. It was noticed that these early food additives had positive side effects, too. Ginger was recognised as being excellent for the digestion, cloves for the sinews, mace for colic and nutmeg for colds.

As we have mentioned, in the time of Richard I (1189-99), there was a revolution in English cooking. In the better-off kitchens, cooks were regularly using ginger, cinnamon, nutmeg, cloves, galingale, a rhizome, cubebs, (a kind of pepper), coriander, cumin, cardamom and aniseed, resulting in highly spiced cooking very similar to India. They also had a *powder fort*, *powder douce* and *powder blanch* as standard spice mixes.

The alehouse first became popular in the thirteenth century, and the first taverns opened in London in 1272, providing a venue for communal eating and drinking and an opportunity for further culinary experimentation. By 1309 there were 354 taverns, proving just how popular this new invention was.

In 1357, *Sauce Blanc*, (basic white sauce, later to be called *béchamel* by the French), was first recorded as the classic *balsamella*, in Cesna, in Italy

The first celebrity chef came from France to work for Edward III (1327 - 1377). Guillaume Tirel, known as *Taillevent*, wrote one of the first major cookery books called *Le Viander* (The Gourmet). Unlike his modern counterparts, Taillevent loved spices and used them extensively.

The museum of Saint Germain has a representation of Taillevant from the sacristy of the Church of Prieure D'Hanemont.

Then, in Richard II's reign (1377-1399) the first real English cookery book was written. Richard employed 200 cooks and they, plus others, including philosophers, produced a work in 1390 containing 196 recipes, called *The Forme of Cury*. *Cury* was the Old English word for cooking derived from the French *cuire* - to cook - hence *cuisine*.

In these early days our European cousins had also begun to colonise all around the world. In 1446 the Portuguese arrived in Guinea-Bissau in Africa, in the person of slave trader Nuno Tristao. But their most famous explorer was Vasco da Gama, who landed in Calicut in southern India in 1498 and brought back cinnamon, cloves, ginger and pepper (see the feature on pages 20-21).

This Portuguese influence led to a trade monopoly, which was strengthened during the period 1509-1515 under Dom Alfonso d'Alberqueque. It was fellow spice-loving Portuguese colonists who introduced or influenced so much of the Goan food that is so popular today: Vindaloo - nothing to with potatoes (aloo), but rather based on the Portuguese words for wine and garlic, *vinho* and *alhos*, both key ingredients in the original recipe. It was the globe-trotting Portuguese who introduced chillies from the Americas into Cochin and Calicut in 1501. By 1543 three varieties were successfully being grown locally. In fact, so unfamiliar were the local people with chilli prior to the coming of the Portuguese, that, for many years, it was known as Goan Pepper.

For many years chilli was known as Goan Pepper

The Iberians kept themselves very busy over the next few years, introducing fruit and vegetables from the New World to the Old. It was the Spanish who brought the tomato from Peru and Mexico to Europe - albeit initially unsuccessfully, after the discovery by early botanists that it was quite closely related to the poisonous Deadly Nightshade. The Portuguese, for their part, took the taro (a root crop), potato, sweet potato and frying in batter (Tempura) to Japan in the sixteenth century.

THE

FORME OF CURY,

A ROLL

OF

ANCIENT ENGLISH COOKERY,

Compiled, about A. D. 1390, by the Master-Cooks of King RICHARD II,

Presented afterwards to Queen ELIZABETH, by EDWARD Lord STAFFORD,

And now in the Possession of GUSTAVUS BRANDER, Esq.

Illustrated with NOTES,

And a copious INDEX, or GLOSSARY.

A MANUSCRIPT of the EDITOR, of the same Age and Subject, with other congruous Matters, are subjoined.

" —— ingeniosa gula est." MARTIAL.

LONDON,

PRINTED BY J. NICHOLS,

PRINTER TO THE SOCIETY OF ANTIQUARIES.

M DCC LXXX.

18

The English Emerge

Following the example of Portugal, Denmark, France and Holland, England, as represented by Elizabeth I, encouraged 'private commerce' to become involved, running alongside the Navy's other quasi-piratical activities. A remarkably realistic woman, Elizabeth saved a lot of money this way. Whilst her Iberian cousins were handing out money to fund Christopher Columbus, she not only got her sailors to pay their own way, but also managed to generate a nice profit for herself at the same time by demanding her share of the spoils. Okay, so in the case of a lot of these 'privateers', some of the loot might not have come *directly* from the New World, having spent the first part of the journey on the slow-moving Spanish Galleons, but let's face it, the Spanish didn't actually get out their doubloons to pay the original owners. In fact, they stole some of the gold that went into making those doubloons from them in the first place.

The first of these private ventures to set out from our shores was launched by the members of the English East India Company, founded in 1600. So when the English merchants landed at Surat in India in 1608 and 1612, then Calcutta 1633, Madras 1640 and Bombay in 1668, the word *cury* had been part of the English language for well over two hundred years. In fact, it was noted that the meal from Emperor Jahangir's kitchens of *dumpukht* - fowl stewed in butter with spices, almond and raisins - served to those merchants in 1612, was very similar to a recipe for English Chicken Pie in a popular cookery book of the time *The English Hus-wife* written by Gervase Markham. Indeed, as we have seen, many of the spices used in Indian cooking had been used and

The Portuguese In India

During the last decade of the 15th century, adventurers from a number of European countries set sail on a quest to discover a new sea route to India and all the riches it contained. In 1492, Columbus, an Italian, set out from Spain in an effort to reach India and, as a staggering tribute to navigation at the time, ended up discovering America.

However, Vasco-da-Gama, a Portuguese sailor, succeeded in his venture. He successfully rounded South Africa and finally landed at the famous port of Calicut in Kerala, Southern India on May 17, 1498. The ruler of Calicut, bearing the hereditary title of Zamorin, welcomed him cordially, and India's troubles with Europe began.

Vasco-da-Gama carried spices from India to Portugal and made some substantial profits. So the Portuguese sent other expeditions to India, establishing trade centres at Calicut, Cochin and Cannanore. The sea route they used went round the Cape of Good Hope in South Africa and so became known as the "Cape Route to India".

Franciso-de-Almedia was the first Governor of the Portuguese possessions in India. He maintained the supreme power of the Portuguese on the sea and confined their activity to trade and commerce. But it was Alfanso-de-Albuquerque who laid the real foundation of Portuguese power in India. An ambitious man, he first came to India in 1503 as the commander of a squadron, and in 1509 was appointed as the Governor of Portuguese affairs in the sub continent.

In November 1510, he captured Goa, then belonging to the Bijapur Sultanate, and made it the capital of Portuguese territories in India, thus establishing the Portuguese influence on Goan cuisine that we see today. He was supposedly kind to Hindus but very cruel to Muslims and treated them as his enemies. Alfanso died in 1515 when the Portuguese were supreme as the strongest naval power in India.

Vasco da Gama from the book by Lisuarte de Abreu, 1558-1564 The Pierpont Morgan Library

After Alfanso, his successors continued to expand their territories. They added Diu, Daman, Salsette, Bassein, Chaul and Bombay, San Thome near Madras and Hooghly in Bengal to their possessions. However, they were not as capable as Alfanso.

Several causes led to the decline of the Portuguese in the sub continent, including religious interference. They also desired, to earn quick profits and so they plundered the Arab ships. With half a eye on their new discoveries in Brazil, they failed to compete successfully with the other European Companies such as the Dutch, French and English, who came in their wake, so they gradually lost all their territories except Diu, Daman and Goa which were retained until 1961.

However, had the Portuguese not discovered and traded in India, it is doubtful we would have chillies in our curries today and what a loss that would be!

21

traded by Europeans for hundreds of years by then.
Britain had wrenched complete mastery in India from the other European
powers, with the last Nawab of Bengal being killed at the battle of Plassey
in 1757. At this time India adopted the chop (although it became a round
potato cake with stuffing), and the cutlet, consisting of meat, chicken or
prawn pounded to a flat oval with the bone sticking out.
Curry powder had been invented along the lines of *garam masala* (spice
mixture) long before in the 17th century, and was very similar to 'kitchen
pepper', a universal English spice mix, which makes an appearance in
English recipes around 1682, the ingredients of which included ginger,
pepper, cloves, nutmegs and cinnamon.

Curry powder had been invented along the lines of garam masala (spice mixture) long before the 17th century, and was very similar to 'kitchen pepper', a spice mix.

And so the British love of curry was well on its way, although mainly in
private households, since dining in restaurants not yet having become
popular.
Many supporters of the Tamil word *kari* as the origin of the word curry,
use the definition from the excellent Hobson-Jobson *Anglo-Indian
Dictionary*, first published in 1886. The book quotes a passage from the
Mahavanso (c AD477, Sri Lanka's oldest chronicle), which says 'he partook
of rice dressed in butter with its full accompaniment of curries.", by way
of proof. The important thing, however, is to note that this is Turnour's
translation of the original *Pali* script, which used the word *supa*; he word
'curry' is not used at all. Indeed Hobson-Jobson even accepts that there is a
possibility that "the kind of curry used by Europeans and Mohommedans
is not of purely Indian origin, but has come down from the spiced cookery
of medieval Europe and Western Asia."

Poem to Curry

Three pounds of veal my darling girl prepares,
And chops it nicely into little squares;
Five onions next procures the little minx
(The biggest are the best, her Samiwel thinks),
And Epping butter nearly half a pound,
And stews them in a pan until they're brown'd.
What's next my dexterous little girl will do?
She pops the meat into the savoury stew,
With curry-powder table-spoonfuls three,
And milk a pint (the richest that may be),
And, when the dish has stewed for half an hour,
A lemon's ready juice she'll o'er it pour.
The, bless her! Then she gives the luscious pot
A very gentle boil - and serves quite hot.
PS - Beef, mutton, rabbit, if you wish,
Lobsters, or prawns, or any kind fish,
Are fit to make a CURRY. 'Tis, when done,
A dish for Emperors to feed upon.

**William Makepeace Thackeray
(from Kitchen Melodies, 1846)**

Authenticity

So, what is this food that everyone calls curry?

Is it even exclusively Indian?

Indian food writers and pundits (another Indian word, by the way), have told us for years that the dishes served in our 'Indian' restaurants over here bear very little resemblance to food served in their homeland. Until quite recently, even asking for a 'curry' on the Indian subcontinent would have caused more than a bit of confusion. Oh yes, they have stew-type dishes of all flavours and hues, but these are not called 'curry; who would describe all Italian food as 'pasta'?

It is interesting to note, in conclusion, that *kari* and *khadi*, (Tamil and north Indian, respectively), meant rice dishes with a relish (sauce) and the Old English word for relish was *kitchen*, which brings us back to our old friend, *cuire*.

When all is said and done, this curry thing is most definitely a British phenomenon.

Whatever the truth, curry, the dish, was rapidly adopted in Britain. In 1747 Hannah Glasse produced the first known recipe for modern *currey* in *Glasse's Art of Cookery*, and by 1773 at least one London Coffee House had curry on the menu. In 1791 Stephana Malcom, the granddaughter of the Laird of Craig included a curry recipe she called Chicken Topperfield plus Currypowder, Chutneys and Mulligatawny soup as recorded in '*In The Lairds Kitchen: Three Hundred Years of Food in Scotland*.

There were also similar 'curries' from the Chinese sector, who, as an interesting aside, invented the very popular British classic of chips and curry sauce, with the help of Butlins holiday camps. The Thais, too, can knock up a great curry. It's even been said, (God forbid), that their green variety could be the new Chicken Tikka Masala.

But when all is said and done, (with great respect to Madhur Jaffrey *et al*), this curry craze is most definitely a British phenomenon. A marriage made, not in heaven, but in the high streets of middle England - not to forget Scotland, Wales and Northern Ireland too!
In 1835, one Lord Marcus Sandys, a former governor of Bengal, returned to England with a recipe for a certain liquor that he felt he could not possible live without in his retirement 'back in Blighty'. He took it to two local chemists in Worcester - a Mr Lea and Mr Perrins, to be exact.
The two chemists made double the quantity, found it to be appalling stuff and hid the surplus away in their cellars. A year or so later, however, further investigation during a spring-clean revealed a very different product indeed.
Over a century-and-a-half later, Worcestershire Sauce is used world-wide in dishes, ranging from Cantonese stir-fries to Spaghetti Bolognese ; Lancashire Hot-Pots to *Hashis Parmentier* (a French version of Shepherd's Pie). However, even in this day and age of extensive food labelling, the exact ingredients are still kept a closely guarded secret, with only four people in the company knowing exactly how much of everything goes into the product.

Lord Sandys took the recipe to two chemists in Worcester - a Mr John Wheeley Lea and a Mr William Henry Perrin .

Before that, in 1809 Dean Mohamet (or Mahomed) from Patna in Bihar, India, had opened the first 'Indian' restaurant dedicated to Indian cuisine. *The Hindostanee Coffee House*, in George Street, London. Aah, you may say, why didn't he call it The Hindostanee *Curry* House? Well, even if you aren't saying it, we're going to tell you anyway. Dean Mohamet was merely following the trend in London at the time to call all such establishments

25

Here we have a Mediaeval recipe by the first celebrity Chef, Guillaume Tirel, or Taillevent, with measurements brought up to date for the modern kitchen.

The only substitution is the use of cider vinegar instead of a popular ingredient of the time called *verjous*, the fermented juice of crab apples, and all the other ingredients would have been available, albeit with some being kept under lock and key! This recipe has been taste-tested by a BBC Radio 4 discussion panel, and they agreed it does actually taste like a modern medium-strength curry. Macrows were an early version of pasta - something like macaroni, but a little rougher in appearance.

Stewed Beef with Macrows

1lb (450g) stewing beef - cubed
1½ pts (570ml) good beef stock
1 carrot, sliced
1 large onion, peeled and finely chopped
1 tsp minced garlic
2 tbsp fresh parsley, chopped
½ tsp dried sage
½ tsp white pepper
1x 2½ " cinnamon stick
½ tsp black peppercorns
½ tsp cloves
2 blades mace
Roughly ground in a pestle and mortar, then place in a muslin bag or spice ball
20ml cider vinegar
2 large slices brown bread, broken up
large pinch saffron, steeped in a little hot water
salt & pepper to taste
generous amount chopped parsley to serve

Method:

Simmer meat, onions, herbs, seasoning and all spices except for
the saffron in the stock, skimming from time to time.

After 1 hour of cooking take ¼pt (150ml) of the stock out of the
pot and mix with the vinegar. Add the crumbled bread and allow
to soak.

When the meat is cooked, add the soaked bread and simmer
until the gravy is thickened.

Add the steeped saffron and cook briefly until colour develops.
Adjust seasoning to taste, sprinkle with fresh parsley and serve
with macaroni.

In this day and age of extensive food labelling, the exact ingredients are still kept a closely guarded secret, with only four people in the company knowing exactly how much of everything goes into the product.

Before that, in 1809 Dean Mohamet (or Mahomed) from Patna in Bihar, India, had opened the first 'Indian' restaurant dedicated to Indian cuisine. *The Hindostanee Coffee House*, in George Street, London. So why didn't he call it The Hindostanee *Curry* House? Dean Mohamet was merely following the trend in London at the time to call all such establishments 'coffee houses' even if they didn't sell coffee. Over 150 years later, his successors in the trade were to follow suit in their own way, making their own curry houses more acceptable to the British public by adopting the red flock wallpaper already so widely in use in pubs and steakhouses. The Hindostanee, however, was very ornate and costs were high such that he had to apply for bankruptcy in 1812.

The lower classes ate 'poor man's food' - oysters. However, Samuel Pepys loved them and used to go out and buy them, pretending that they were for his cat.

Another factor in the restaurant's failure was probably the fact that eating out wasn't a big thing at the time. The richer residents of London all employed their own kitchen staff, some of whom were very fancy French chefs indeed, brought in at great expense to impress. The other classes? Well, they were eating what was regarded then as 'poor man's food' oysters. Samuel Pepys loved them, apparently. However, he used to go out and buy them himself, pretending that they were for his cat, as his servant was too ashamed to do it for him.

In spite of this initial setback in introducing Indian food to London, and the fact that French cooks were, once again, taking a stranglehold in the grand kitchens, by 1850, curry was well established. Queen Victoria, who had an Indian confidant, Abdul Karim, is said to have had a curry prepared every day by two Indian chefs in the event she had a visitor from

The First Man Of Curry

Dean Mahomet (also referred to as Mahomed) was born in 1759 in Patna, in Bihar, East India of a middle class Bengali family. His father reached rank of subadar in the Company's Bengal Army, the second highest rank that an Indian could hold at the time. Dean's father died in 1769 somewhat prematurely and the young Dean was befriended by a cadet named Godfrey Evan Baker from Cork. As Baker rose in the ranks he carried Dean along with him so he grew up in the strange world of neither being completely Indian nor European.

In 1784 Baker was dismissed the service and returned to Cork taking the twenty five year old Dean with him. Such was Baker's position in the Anglo-Irish elite that Dean had immediate access to the right people and soon made a position for himself. He set about advancing his education and began writing *The Travels of Dean Mohamet* which became the first book written and published by an Indian in English in 1794. In 1786 Baker died and Dean any curries ever made in England with choice wines and every accommodation". The chairs were made from bamboo and Indian and Chinese pictures adorned the

29

walls. Mahomet eloped with, then married, Jane Daly, having to post a substantial wedding bond at the church.

Soon after the turn of the century he moved to London with Jane and his 10 year old son William and took up a position with the Honourable Basil Cochrane in Portman Square, London. Here he helped Cochrane develop his 'vapour bath' (some say it was to Mahomet's design) and introduced "shampooing"(therapeutic massage, later to become aromatherapy). Unfortunately Dean Mahomet received little acknowledgement for his inventions so, in 1809 he continued his promotion of things Indian by opening *The Hindostanee Coffee House* at 34 George Street, behind Cochrane's Portman Square house.

The restaurant was smart and designed to appeal to the nobility and gentry, and was advertised as 'being for the entertainment of Indian gentlemen where they may enjoy the Hoakha, with real Chilm tobacco and Indian dishes, in the highest perfection, and allowed by the greatest epicures to be unequalled to, emphasising the 'Oriental' connections.

The restaurant and its cuisine were well received but the necessary repeat custom was hard to develop, as most big houses connected with India had their own kitchen with their own Indian staff, and Portman Square was well away from the fashionable coffee house haunts of the City. He took on John Spencer as a partner but in 1812 had to apply for bankruptcy due to the high start-up costs and slow development of custom.

It was to be almost one hundred years before the next Indian

Dean Mohamet in Regency dress

He moved to Brighton with his family and soon created Mahomed's Bath House

restaurant was opened in England, heralding the amazing growth of the last century, making Dean Mahomet very much a man before his time.

He moved on to Brighton with his family now including William, Amelia (b.1808), Henry Edwin (b. 1810) and Deen (b. 1812), and such was his resilience that he had soon created Mahomed's Bath House where he promoted and practiced the art of 'shampooing' based on the Indian arts of 'champi and malish'. By 1815 he claimed to have treated a thousand cases and Jane gave birth to Rosanna as the Mahomed's, as they were now called, received a royal warrant as 'Shampooing Surgeon' to King George IV and King William IV. The remarkable Dean Mahomet eventually died in 1851 in his ninety-second year with failing fortunes but a life full of achievement and determination to survive and grow. He was the first Indian to be published in English, the man who brought shampooing and aromatherapy to England and is the father of the British Indian restaurant and curry industry and deserves recognition as such.

Abdul Karim (Munshi)

India. Abdul Karim became the Queen's favourite and most favoured servant, often being referred to as her 'Munshi'. He remained close to her during all her travels until she died in 1901, when he was allowed to walk with the funeral procession. He finally returned to Agra in northern India where he died at the age of 46 in 1909. During this century, migrating Hindus started settling in other countries around the world, taking their cooking and spices as far afied as the West Indies, creating the influences on Caribbean cuisine we see today.

As the 19th century progressed, another glitch in the matchmaking process between curry and fan emerged. Unrest fomented throughout India, resulting in the revolts by the Sikhs of Pubjab in 1845 and 1846, which caused 2,500 British casualties. Although eventually defeated in 1849, these events saw the beginning of disenchantment with the subcontinent back in Britain.

In 1857, the famous Sepoy Mutiny near Delhi began under the banner of Bahadur Shah II, the last of the Mughal Emperors. Europeans were massacred and siege was laid to the British Residency in Lucknow. The uprising was put down in 1859, ending the final chapter of Mughal history in India, and the British Government assumed control of the country from the East India Company.

Further trouble in India

This further alienated British public opinion, whatever the rights and wrongs of the situation. Feelings were also heightened by the spread of Indian nationalism, with acts of terrorism by a few, and acts of mass repression by the British. In 1885, the India National Congress was founded and further fanned the flames of revolt, and by the early years of the 20th century British goods were being banned in India.

Thus the love affair with all things Indian, particularly the food, which had been so obvious up to the mid 19th century, started to come to an end. In cooking terms, the growing interest in Indian food was completely eclipsed by French cuisine, which was already popular. This, together with the obvious disruption and supply problems caused by two world wars, ensured the almost complete disappearance of soicy food, which continued, with few exceptions, right up until the 1960s.

You (the British) conquered us with gunpowder, now we have conquered you - with curry powder'.

This state of affairs wasn't to last though. Strong foundations had been laid for its reappearance and once the aftermath of World War II had been dealt with and mass immigration had started in Britain, Indian cooking wasn't going to go away again. As the former Bangladeshi High Commissioner, AH Mahmood Ali said in 1999: 'You (the British) conquered us with gunpowder, now we have conquered you - with curry powder.'

In the relatively short space of fifty years, the Indian restaurant has become part of the very fabric of British life. On high streets, in converted toilets, in old pubs and even in onetime churches, the Indian restaurant has appeared wherever there is a community to be served.

The transformation from the first Indian restaurant in Britain in 1809 to the present day situation of one - at least - on every High Street in the land, as well as on our highways, byways and even remote Scottish islands, is a long story of hardship, endeavour, application, an inimitable willingness to adapt and, ultimately, succeed.

The story of British involvement with India began with the almost casual first visit by the armed merchant ships of the English East India Company to Surat in North West India in 1608. India was not, of course, the real destination, but the commercial jewel of the East Indies and its wonderful spices. It was fate, in the shape of the Dutch East India Company and the so-called Amboyne Massacre in 1623, that took a hand. This was a convincing display of violence, in which the Dutch wiped out all the officers of the other European nations' delegations in the area, and which caused the English to accept Dutch dominance in the region and turn their full attention to India instead.

India was not the real destination but the spice rich islands of the East Indies.

East India Company Coat of Arms

Soon lascars - seamen, mainly from Bengal - were helping to man British ships and, despite The Navigation Act of 1660, stating that 75% of the crew of a British ship had to be British, a number of lascars began appearing in London throughout the 17th century. IThe population of London had increased in the sixteenth century to 250,000 souls, with cookshops, inns and alehouses to provide food and drink. The cookshops were the forerunners of the snack bar and restaurant and were located in Bread Street, Eastcheap and similar areas. At the other end of the scale, lavish meals and ceremonial banquets were organised by the livery companies, the real power in the city at the time, and the City of London alone, the famous 'square mile' had 1,000 alehouses in which to obtain a square meal, by 1613.

This period also saw the quite rapid change from medieval to Renaissance, moving into a new era of commerce and amenity provision Taverns, already a natural meeting place for the masses, with three hundred years experience of catering to the traveller, added a new dimension and became places where traders and businessmen could meet. Even the poor were catered for, albeit less grandly; cookshops providing basic cooking services for the overcrowded and poorly equipped Londoners of the day, and street hawkers, touting foodstuffs for those on the move.

Eating habits change

Lunch had been the main meal for centuries, but by 1660 it had moved to mid/late afternoon, presumably a natural movement towards a more social event rather than a mere refuelling of the body. The first hallmarked fork appeared in 1632, showing a tendency to adapt to a more graceful eating style, (and, more importantly, to get food past those annoying neck ruffs), and 'ordinaries' - embryonic restaurants - appeared, offering fixed-price meals.

In 1652, Pasqua Rosée, a Ragusian man-servant, opened the first public coffee house in St Michael's Alley, Cornhill, in the City of London, an achievement that is also ascribed to one Christopher Bowman in some quarters. This proved so successful that by the following year there were 63 in the city, serving coffee from Turkey and the Middle East with names like the Turks Head. Tipping also started at around this time, from the practice of putting money in a box in order to ensure prompt service. The first tea advertisement – announcing the sale of "China Tcha, Tay or Tee" – appeared on 30 September 1658, in the newspaper *Mercurius Politicus*,

booked by the owner of The Sultaness Head Coffee House.
Despite clients being expected to load the tipping box, such establishments
as Jonathon's, Button's, Lloyds and Will's soon became the meeting place
for all professions within the City. Lloyd's Coffee House, in Tower Street,
became the place where the owners and insurers of commercial ships and
their cargoes would meet
in order to conduct
business. Eventually,
Lloyds Coffee House
became the now famous
insurance exchange,
Lloyd's of London.
Londoners were really
taking to 'doing lunch'
now, and luxury Eating

Houses began to open, especially after the influx of the protestant
Hugenots, escaping religious persecution in France, in 1680.

The first restaurants

The earliest use of the word 'restaurant' was by the French poet, Clement
Marot, in the early sixteenth century, to refer to a group of fortifying meat
broths. In 1765, however, a man named Boulanger set up a business to
avoid the Guild monopoly on the sale of broths, by offering 'restaurants' -
ragouts - on his own premises, instead. He served up his 'restaurants' on
little marble tables without cloth, with a further choice of poached poultry
with coarse salt, fresh eggs and broth, the word soon became synonymous
with food served in this way, and the restaurant was born.
Eighteenth century Britain was a time of new money and flourishing
commerce. The Middle Class tradesmen were acquiring more disposable

income and were looking around at ways in which to dispose of it. One of the most natural and, of course, pleasurable, was on entertainment and food. Recipe books were published to cater to a newly fired interest of the ladies of that class in the affairs of the kitchen; eating houses flourished in response; Coffee Houses began to offer food. A new concept was introduced in the Chop Houses, specialising in guess what chops and meat, (and the forerunner of the modern bottled brown sauce chop sauce). Food gained a new importance and beef was seen as a sign of strength and prosperity. This era, more than the Tudor, was a time of excess, in terms of food consumption, with corpulent landowners, squires, and even clergymen succumbing to that scourge of the glutton gout. Even then, some saw this accumulation of excess weight as a problem, and moderation was recommended by health experts of the time. Ladies started to join in the fun, with inns becoming unisex, but taverns remained men only. However, the diet for the poor was still bread, cheese and pie. As the influence of the British in India grew, so did the interest in Indian food back in Britain, leading to the publishing of recipes and the commercial creation of curry powder in 1780. The first appearance of curry on a menu was at the Coffee House in Norris Street, Haymarket, London in 1773.

By 1804 the number of lascars in London was quoted as being 471 and yet by 1810 it had risen to over 1400, around 130 of which would die each year, such was the poor condition of their circumstances.

A letter dated 28 November 1809 from Hilton Docker, medical doctor to the lascars, describes vividly their condition, both on board ship, and in England:

"The Natives of India who come to this country are mostly of bad constitutions. Numbers are landed sick from the ships, where they have been ill, and when they arrive (usually at the latter end of the year) they have to encounter with a climate and season to

them particularly pernicious which most frequently increase their disease. Those who are landed in health are of course exposed to the same danger of climate and season and in addition almost all of them give way to every excess in drinking and debauchery, and contact to a violent degree those diseases (particularly venereal) which such habits are calculated to produce."

Concern about their plight led to the creation of The Society for the Protection of Asiatic Sailors in 1814, and in 1869 a complaint was made to the India Office in London that there were upwards of 400 destitute Asians on the streets. During this time Britain saw many people from India visit her shores ranging from be-jewelled princes to humble manservants, but the opening of the first, though short-lived Indian restaurant in 1809 (see chapter one) marked a watershed that was to take over one hundred years to start to come to fruition.

The only eating establishments offering Indian cuisine were community meeting places.

As the twentieth century dawned, the only eating establishments offering Indian cuisine were community meeting places for those who had jumped ship in London looking for a new life or, more often, been put ashore without any means of support. Some of these were *Vandary* (Indian chefs) who jumped ship to seek work in London's small but growing restaurant community, but these were not enough to provide any real impetus for the cuisine.

In 1830 Alexis Soyer was one of the many French chefs who came to Britain, and his thinking influenced British dining for many years. The nineteenth century saw the arrival of restaurants and hotels in Britain, with celebrity chefs such as Ude, Francatelli and Escoffier, who introduced the a la carte style of dining during his twenty years at the London Carlton from 1899. Three establishments in Leicester Square alone in 1815 were described as 'French restaurants'.

The only eating establishments offering Indian cuisine were community meeting places for those who had jumped ship in London.

Georges Auguste Escoffier

Concern about food adulteration led to the 1875 Sale of Food and Drugs Act, leading to a great improvement in quality by 1880. This was to combat the practice of 'padding out' various ingredients to increase profit margins and required the clear labelling of processed foods with a full list of ingredients. These early food additives ranged from chalk in flour and bread, to mushroom ketchup being made from rotting horse livers. One source, (R. Shipperbottom , *The Adulteration of Spices* 1993), reveals that mustard in the 1850s contained only a marginal amount of the seed, the rest being made up of flour, linseed meal and plaster of Paris, coloured with turmeric and spiced with cayenne pepper and we worry about E-numbers!

The sandwich had been invented by John Montagu, the 4th Earl of Sandwich around a hundred years before this, as a means of eating without leaving his card games, and had become very popular.

41

Meanwhile, some eating houses started to specialise in 'fried fish in the Jewish fashion', served with baked potato, a popular street food at the time. It was only a short step to frying the potatoes for speed's sake that would herald the birth of the famous British fish and chip industry. Chips, called 'pommes frites or french fries' in many countries, were, in fact native to Belgium but supposedly misnamed in World War I when American soldiers encountered them and believed their trenches to be France when they were actually in Belgium.

The aristocracy arrive

Meanwhile, unrest and political machinations back on the Indian sub-continent, also saw plenty of immigrants at the upper end of the social scale, often glamorous members of Royal families, keeping up the interest in all things Indian. One such was the exiled Maharaja of the Punjab, Duleep Singh, who lived in Britain from 1854 to 1886. He was a favourite of Queen Victoria, who was herself an Indiaphile, and lived in the splendid country house Elvedon Hall in Suffolk. In 1886, he fell out with the British Government. It wasn't too bad when the salary rise he applied for was refused. The last straw was the refusal of the British Government to return the *Koh-i-Noor* diamond him. It was obtained by the British when the Punjab was annexed in 1849 and presented to the Queen to mark the 250th anniversary of the East India Company.

Duleep   Singh

42

Perhaps his friendship with the Queen might have endured a little longer and he might even have got his pay rise - if only he hadn't wanted to take away the most fabulous diamond in her collection. He left England in a marked manner and eventually died in Paris in 1893.

Indian immigration and integration into British life started quite early and almost certainly because of the involvement of the East India Company. For example: one of the first Anglo-Indian marriages was in Deptford in 1613; the first recorded case of an Indian being baptised was recorded on 22nd December, 1616 at St Dionis Backchurch in the City of London and was celebrated in the presence of governors of the East India Company presumably an indication that the baptism was of one of the many servants and retainers brought back to this country by their agents.

Indian faces were a familiar sight to 18th century Londoners; parish records from many districts reflect that they were a growing sector of the community. The main reason for this was that many unscrupulous ex-patriots, employing servants to accompany them on their journey home with a promise to return them to India, simply dumped them on arrival, leaving them to fend for themselves.

By the late 18th century Indians were employed as servants and *ayahs* (nannies) to the ruling classes. Apart from the fact that servants from the sub-continent were significantly cheaper to employ than their English counterparts, they also added to the mystique of a returning English 'Nabob', underlining his importance. Although many of these were returned home to India, some stayed after their service, and other British cities soon found a similar influx of Indians into their community. Edinburgh, Cheltenham and Bath, all cities with populations containing a high percentage of the British elite, gained a small population of Indians in this way.

Joining the establishment

As mentioned previously, the first 'curry house' was opened by Dean Mohammet in 1809, and the first mosque in 1889 in Woking. More significantly, however, was the election of the first Asian Member of Parliament, Dadabhai Naoroji, in 1892. The "Grand Old Man of India", as he was affectionately known, was born in Bombay in 1825, the son of a Parsi priest. He attended Elphinstone College, Bombay, and became a professor of Mathematics and Natural Philosophy there, aged 27; he was the first Indian to become a professor of the college. Three years later he left for England, where he was to spend most of his life trying to influence public opinion for Indian self-rule and writing about the plight of the people of his homeland. He lost an election to the British Parliament as a member of the Liberal party in 1886, mainly

Dadabhai Naoroji

due to opposition and resistance to the election of a 'black man' within the party itself. Success came, however, with the backing of the mainly white working class population of Central Finsbury, North London - still standing as a Liberal. He died in 1916 aged 91.

Three years later, in 1895, another Indian, Mancherjee Bhownaggree, was elected to Parliament. Despite the fact that he was a Tory, a far more aggressively conservative party than its modern descendant, he was elected by white workers in the east London constituency of Bethnal Green.

The first Asian cricketer appeared in the English team in 1895. Ranjitsinhji, (Ranji, as he was known to his friends), or, more formally, H.H. the Maharajah Jam Sahib of Nawanagar, never played for India, but is said to

44

have been ultimately responsible for spreading the game's popularity in India. He played for Cambridge University, Sussex, and between 1896 and 1902 for England. In 1899, he was the first batsman to reach 3,000 runs in an English season. Ranjitsinhji played his last test for England, in 1902. Colonel Shri Sir Ranjitsinghji Vibhaji (1872-1933) was reputed to be one of the world's best cricketers, and the author of The Jubilee Book of Cricket. Although he lost an eye in a shooting accident, he continued playing cricket to show that it was possible to bat with only one eye'. With growing influence and

Colonel Shri Sir Ranjitsinghji Vibhaji

visibility of Indian people in Britain, Indian food soon followed. The first recorded Indian restaurant of the twentieth century was the *Salut e Hind* (Hail to India) in Holborn in 1911 but the first to have any real influence was *Shafi's* opened by Mohammed Wayseem and Mohammed Rahim in 1920. Coming from North India, they opened their cafe in London's Gerard Street (now the centre of London's Chinatown), and employed four or five ex-seamen. It soon became a kind of community and Indian Student Centre, a welcome addition for the growing number of Indian students in the UK, whose numbers had risen from 100 in 1880 to 1,800 by 1931.

With the growing influence and visibility of Indian people in Britain, Indian food soon followed.

At the same time things were happening in India where Haji Karimuddin, a descdent of the cooks who had worked for the Mughal emperors, opened his Karim in 1913 near The Red Fort. K.K.Rao opened Woodlands in Madras in 1930s to introduce South Indian food to the up-market restaurant scene.

Soon *The Shafi* was taken over by Dharam Lal Bodua and run by an English manager, with employees such as Israil Miah and Gofur Miah, who were later to run their own establishments. One of Dharam's great friends was one Bir Bahadur from Delhi who opened *The Kohinoor* in Roper Street (pulled down in 1978), and who was to have a major influence on the industry.

These restaurants were mainly for Asians, - although Shafi certainly had a mixed clientele - but in 1927 the first fashionable Indian restaurant opened when Edward Palmer, launched *Veeraswamy's Indian Restaurant* in London's Regent Street, where it still thrives today, owned by husband and wife team, Ranjit Mathrani and Namita Panjabi. A well-connected Anglo-Indian, Palmer's great-grandfather was Lieutenant General William Palmer, principal secretary to Warren Hastings, the first Viceroy of India, and his great-grandmother was the daughter of the Nizam of Hyderabad.

Edward Palmer

Above : The popular Shafi which opened in   1920

Below : Veeraswamy's as it was in 1927, the first really fashionable Indian restaurant in Britain.

Above : Shafi's influenced others such as Israil and Gofur Miah and Bir Bahadur to opene their own restaurants.

Below : Veeraswamy's in 1927 very much reflected the glory of the Raj

Veeraswamy's became called 'The ex-Indian higher serviceman's curry club'.

Edward had been greatly encouraged by friends and acquaintances after his successful running of the *Mughal Palace* in The Empire Exhibition at the brand new Wembley Stadium in 1924. He brought staff from India and created such a traditional atmosphere that it became called "The ex-Indian higher serviceman's curry club".

Many of the people from all over India who were later to become the backbone of the new 'curry' restaurant industry, learned their trade at Veeraswamy's.

In due course Veeraswamy's was sold to Sir William Steward, M.P., who ran the restaurant for 40 years. He travelled the world in order to source produce and was dubbed 'the curry king' by The Times. His other claim to fame is the introduction of curry in a can. The name of the restaurant was changed to The Veeraswamy during ownership by Sarova Hotels and to Veeraswamy under the present ownership.

The Indian restaurant takes root

Meanwhile Sordar and Shomsor Bahadur had come from India to join their brother and opened *The Taj Mahal*, Brighton; *Taj Mahal*, Oxford; *Taj Mahal* Northampton; *Kohinoor*, Cambridge; *Kohinoor*, Manchester, all before the outbreak of the Second World War and mainly staffed by ex-seamen. Such was the influence of the Bahadur family that it was estimated that nearly all first-generation East Pakistani (now Bangladeshi) restaurateurs learned their trade from the Bahadur brothers.

Other cafés for the seamen, usually from the province of Sylhet, East Bengal (modern Bangladesh), opened throughout the years between the wars; establishments such as Abdul Rashim and Koni Khan's coffee shop, serving curry and rice on Victoria Dock Road around 1920.

Gradually the development of Indian restaurants spread outwards from London between the two world wars, and many of the restaurants that have influenced those established today were created. Amongst those in London pre- 1939 were *The Durbar* on Percy Street owned by Asuk Mukerjee from Calcutta, and his compatriot from the same city Nogandro Goush, who owned *The Dilkush* in Windmill Street.

Gradually the development of Indian restaurants spread outwards from London

Abdul Gofur opened a café shop at 120 Brick Lane, as well as others in New Road and Commercial Road, and Ayub Ali Master came back from America in 1938 and opened *Shah Jalal* on Commercial Street London. *Shirref's* in Great Castle Street opened in 1935 and *Halal*, which still thrives today, opened in St Mark's Street, London E1 in 1939.

Many cafes opened up around the seaports of Britain by ex-seamen, but they had great difficulty in obtaining the necessary rice and spices.

During the Second World War the community social focus shifted to *The Gathor*, a basement café at 36 Percy Street, London, but soon after Sanu Miah opened *The Green Mask* on Brompton Road, which became a centre for prominent East Pakistanis and their politicians. Also in 1942-3 Mosrof Ali and Israil Miah opened *The Anglo Asian* at 146 Brompton Road, London. In 1956 Mosrof Ali had also opened *The Durbar* in Hereford Road, London W2, which is still run by his family today, now back in its original location after a sojourn in nearby Westbourne Grove following a closure due to fire.

The fifties and sixties saw a rapid growth in Indian restaurant numbers in Britain, especially London and the South East, where over 45% of all Indian restaurants in the UK are still located. Gradually the Indian restaurant concept spread all over Britain, even though those running the restaurants were often not Indian at all. Until Bangladeshi Independence in 1971 at least three quarters of 'Indian' restaurants in Britain were Pakistani-owned.

Durbar in Hereford Street

The 1950s and 1960s saw a rapid growth in Indian restaurant numbers

After 1971, the geographical differences became clear, with over half the restaurants owned and managed by Bangladeshis, most of whom were from the one region of Sylhet, located in northeast Bangladesh, near the border with the Indian province of Assam.

In Birmingham Abdul Aziz opened a café shop selling curry and rice in

51

Steelhouse Lane in 1945, which became *The Darjeeling*, the first Indian restaurant in Birmingham, owned by Afrose Miah. The second was *The Shah Bag* on Bristol Street, but growth really got underway in the 1950's. Manchester's curry scene started with the Bahadur brother's *Kohinoor* in Oxford Street followed by Malik Bokth with *The Everest*, Nojir Uddin who opened *Monzil* and Lal Miah who opened *The Orient*. *Rajdoot*, long a favourite in Manchester, opened in 1966.

In Bradford, *The Sweet Centre* on Lumb Lane, which opened in 1964, was one of the earliest after *The Kashmir* in Morley Street in 1958. When the owner of *The Shafi*, Mr Dharan died in 1963, Ahmed Kutub, who worked there, went to open his own restaurant in Newcastle and, in the 1950s, Rashid Ali moved from a café shop in London's Drummond Street to Cardiff, to open his own establishment.

It was estimated that nearly all first-generation East Pakistani (now Bangladeshi) restaurateurs learned their trade from the Bahadur brothers.

North of the border, the first record is of a restaurant opened in Glasgow by Dr Deb from Nawakhali before 1939. However, many claim the first was The Taj Mahal in Park Road which was opened in 1954 by Sultan Ahmed Ansari whose family still claim he was the inventor of Chicken Tikka Masala. There you could have a feast for just over 3 shillings (15p today).

Edinburgh too was at the forefront with the opening of Kushi's in 1947. So the Indian restaurant spread all over Britain, fuelled by an enthusiastic, but barely trained, workforce with their eyes firstly on survival and, later on, riches.

The amazing Empire Exhibition at Wembley in 1924 bringing the mysteries of India and the Orient to the British public.
(Photos courtesy of Pye's of Clitheroe)

In the sixties and seventies, owners began to make serious money from the industry, with people such as Rajiv Ali, now Chairman of the South East Bank in Bangladesh, having found his fortune with a curry house on Whitechapel Road, London E1. Haji Abdul Razzah came to Britain with an early wave of immigrants and lived in Kentish Town in 1960. He opened The Polash in Shoeburyness near Southend (which still flourishes) and returned to Bangladesh in 1985 and bought *The Polash Hotel* in Sylhet having made his fortune from 'chicken tikka masala'.

The introduction of lager to Indian restaurants was accidental.

The Indian restaurant culture continued to spread, fuelled by the beer culture, and Indian food became synonymous with lager. Strangely enough, the introduction of lager to Indian restaurants was accidental and owes its history, not to a British or Indian product, but a Danish one. The Prince of Denmark was visiting his sister, Queen Mary, wife of George V, soon after the opening of Veerswamy's in 1927 and decided to dine at the restaurant taking with him his drink of choice - Carlsberg. Fifty years later, almost all licensed Indian restaurants stocked the brand until the introduction of Kingfisher lager from India in the 1980's, to be followed closely by Cobra, Lal Toofan and other smaller brands.

The tandoor

Perhaps the most influential thing in the development of the Indian restaurant in this country, however, was the introduction of the tandoor oven(see feature on pages 58-59).

Above : Chutney Mary in Chelsea

Below : The fascinating Chor Bizarre in Mayfair

An ancient cooking method, using a large, pot-bellied clay oven, it introduced yet another new taste dimension to the British palate, producing smoky-flavoured, succulent food items with exotic names such as tikka and kebabs, which were not too spicy and appeared at the table very quickly, due to the speed of cooking.

Ironically, as far as the restaurant is concerned, the tandoor had been a fairly recent innovation even in India itself. Although having been long used in some communities in northern India as a communal bakery, in modern times, the first tandoor in India in a restaurant is said to have been at the Kashmiri *Moti Mahal,* in New Delhi, in 1948. Kundan Lal came from Peshawar and he opened Moti Mahal near The Red Fort in 1947. He worked with a local man to produce the restaurant version of the village tandoor and then invented the tandoori spice mix for tandoori chicken that is still used today - ground coriander seeds, black pepper and mild red pepper.

Ranjit Mathrani, director of *Chutney Mary* and *Veeraswamy,* in London, remembers eating tandoori food there in 1951 at the tender age of eight. Several restaurants have claimed to be the first to have a tandoor in Britain. Initial research had suggested the man responsible was, in fact, Mahendra Kaul who started the excellent *Gaylord* group and it was The Gaylord in Mortimer Street who advertised it in a Palladium Theatre programme in 1966. Mr Kaul had taken the tandoor to America for the Worlds Fair in 1964, then loaned it and his staff to a restaurant in Whitfield Street, London that no longer exists, before starting the Gaylord. He is still a partner in *Chor Bizarre* in London, making him one of the most experienced people still working in the industry.

Archived documents at Veeraswamy indicate, however, that a tandoor was in use much earlier, in 1959. So, once again, this famous restaurant seems to have been ahead of the rest, having also been responsible for the earliest introduction of tandoori style dishes to the UK, although it would be some ten years and more before the tandoor became widely used in Britain. If you had visited Veerawamy's, as it was then called, in December 1959 you could have enjoyed Chicken Tandoori (allow 15-20 minutes) for the princely sum of ten shillings and sixpence, (£7.27 converting to modern values).

Chicken Tandoori would have cost you the princely sum of 10 shillings and 6 pence.

There is no denying that the introduction of the tandoor was to be a turning point for the Indian restaurant in the UK. As restaurateurs started to bring the ovens over to the U.K., restaurant names began changing to incorporate the word 'tandoori'. Between 1960 and 1970, Indian restaurant numbers grew from 500 nationwide to 1,200 and most of them called tandooris.

Today, the tandoor is in use all over Britain and wherever the Indian restaurant industry thrives, as well as in its countries of origin, and commercial tandoors now have cemented brick walls with brushed steel cladding, and large commercial units are made of iron. However, Mohammed Aslam, director and executive chef of the Aagrah Group in Yorkshire, explained that many Pakistani and Kashmiri restaurants in Britain continue to use the tandoor for breads only, preferring to grill their kebabs. Elsewhere, others are expanding the use of the versatile tandoor to give that special flavour to meat and fish.

The Ubiquitous Tandoor

The Punjab in India is regarded by many today as being the 'home of the tandoor, a cooking method that has become known all over the world as the popularity of 'curry' has spread. Its history, however, actually goes back to the dawn of civilisation, from where it spread from Arab countries to India and finally, the West.

The tandoor in its simplest form is a large clay jar, with an opening at the bottom for adding and removing fuel. Originally used for bread baking, where the dough was slapped onto the vertical wall to bake quickly by radiant heat and convection. It was traditionally made of good clay and shredded coir rope, with a paste of mustard oil, jaggery (palm sugar), yoghurt and ground spinach rubbed on the inside to harden it up.

In Afghanistan, the tandoor was usually built into the ground, and was a communal oven. Households would prepare their

own dough and take it to the tandoor bakery (nanwaee) to be baked. Notches were worked into a stick called a chobe khat, totalling the number of breads baked for a household each week for payment.

The word tandoor came originally from the Middle East, being derived from the Babylonian word 'tinuru', in turn from the Semitic word nar, meaning fire. Hebrew and Arabic then made it tannur then tandur in Turkey, Central Asia and, finally Pakistan and India, who exported it Understandably, as this happened very early on in history, many people assume the tandoor to be native to India, as evidence exists of early tandoors there in 3,000 BC.

Although India was first populated around 250,000 years ago, the first major civilization was the Harappan, who farmed Harappa and Mohenjodero in the Indus Valley. By 3,000 B.C. turmeric, cardamom, pepper and mustard were all being harvested in India, attracting trade. They were of mixed stock, somewhat larger in stature than either the Sumerians or Egyptians, countering theories that they were an outpost of those communities. They had club wheat, barley, sheep and goats from the Iranian Plateau and cotton from Southern Arabia or North East Africa, but were held back by their reliance on floodwaters, due to a general lack of knowledge of irrigation.

Sumer had trade links with the Indus Valley, via Hindu Kush by 3,000 B.C., introducing the tandoor amongst many other things, adding sea routes from 2,500 B.C., thus linking the Harappans with both Sumerians and Egyptians in the trade maps of the time.

The tandoor was introduced to restaurants in the Moti Mahal in New Delhi in 1948 after a special restaurant version of the communal cooking method was designed.

At Chor Bizarre, the upmarket restaurant in Albemarle Street, Mayfair, they've gone even further with the experimentation. Mahendra Kaul, one of those early tandoor pioneers, can still be seen today on occasion with partner Rohit Khatar, extolling the virtues of tandoori pineapple, a delicious dessert creation by his chef, Deepinder Singh Sondhi.

Many Pakistani and Kashmiri restaurants use the tandoor for breads only.

To capitalise on the popularity created by this exciting new cooking method, the canny restaurateurs set up comfy, parlour-like rooms, generally with red-flock wallpaper and velour seating - also to be found in the very popular steak houses of the time. In an almost subconscious effort to court further acceptability, restaurant names not only had the now obligatory 'tandoori', many also bore the name of the town or street in which they were located.

The world of entertainment played its part, too, in providing easily recognised and catchy names for new ventures: *Passage to India* and *Jewel in the Crown* soon became firm favourites in high streets up and down the land even as cinema queues were forming to view the films which shared their name.

The menus listed popular British dishes such as prawn cocktail, tomato soup and chicken and chips alongside the more exotic, 'tikka' and 'kebabs', the hallmark of Indian cuisine in Britain, gradually edging out the 'safer' British dishes, until challenged by the balti craze emanating from Birmingham.

mainly to its cost-effective nature. Balti houses did the unthinkable in marketing practice they actually went downmarket: Formica or glass-topped tables, on which were served blackened metals bowls containing a cheap stew to be eaten with naan bread scoops.

Balti houses did the unthinkable in marketing practice - they went downmarket.

Competition raged amongst restaurants to see who could make the largest naans, with some restaurants boasting specimens of up to a yard long! Arguments raged within the sector as to the validity of a cooking style called 'balti' (see feature on pages 62-63). "It's a bucket " said purists and, indeed, according to the Oxford English Dictionary, that is exactly what it is.

Baltis were accompanied by tasty naan bread which gradually became larger and larger until giant naans were the norm.

What Is A Balti?

Balti certainly exists, despite its many detractors, who say the word means 'bucket' - and one would that would be used for rather unsavoury things at that!

This exciting style, which is basically karahi cooking, crept up on the unsuspecting Birmingham in the seventies, and went national in the 'eighties and early 'nineties, and has become so popular that the word is now even listed in the Oxford English Dictionary. The balti pan is a round-bottomed, wok-like, cast iron dish with two handles, roughly nine inches in diameter. Introduced by the many people of Kashmiri origin in Birmingham, provenance for the 'authenticity' of the style was that it hailed from an area once called Baltistan, now in disputed Pakistani Kashmir. It is from here that an ancient people called the Balti hail, and where this wok style of fast cooking is said to have its home.

Baltistan is real. It is a complex of beautiful valleys, situated amid the famous ranges of Himalaya and Karakoram, straddling the River Indus, between Ladakh and Gilgit, including some of the highest peaks of the world in its landscape. The dimensions of Baltistan have been fluctuating over the course of history. It is currently smaller than ever before, with an area of 17,000 square kms. with an estimated population of 400,000.

The first historical reference to the area appears in Ptolemy's BYALTAE - dating back to the 2nd century BC. The Chinese have named it Palolo, Palilo and Palor. The people themselves refer to their homeland as Balti-yul (Land of Baltis) which suggests a link with Ptolemy's BYALTAE. In 727 AD Baltistan was invaded by Tibet and remained Tibetan until 900 AD. It was many centuries before Islam was introduced and in 1840 AD the Dogras of Jammu conquered Baltistan and annexed it to their State. Finally, in 1947-48 AD the area was annexed to Pakistan.

The population of Baltistan is a mixture of ethnic groups. Tibetans form the principal ethnic group in the area accounting for 60 per cent of the population. The language spoken by the entire population of Baltistan is called BALTI - which is an archaic dialect of Tibetan language. The

English Bible was even translated into Balti in the 1930's

Unfortunately that is where the provenance breaks down. There is no evidence that balti cooking comes from this area or that they gave their flat bottomed woks the same name as their language - Balti. After all, Americans don't call their barbecues an America, and Britain's favourite breakfast is not cooked in a Britain! When looking at balti words such as Zo (eat), Thung (drink), Kha (mouth), Byango (chicken), Bras (rice), Tsong (onion), the provenance becomes even shakier.

Wherever it came from, the Birmingham balti is hugely popular and the thousands who throng to the Balti Triangle every night couldn't care less about its background and that is 'chadkha' (a certainty)!

Whatever its provenance, its entry into Europe began in the Sparkhill, Ladypool Road and Sparkbrook areas of Birmingham, in the mid 1970s. Some fans claim to remember the dish, originally aimed at the impoverished student community, introduced in the late 1960s by some farsighted pioneers in those same areas.

There were arguments as to the validity of a cooking style called 'balti' which literally means 'bucket'

There were around 50 balti houses in the 'Balti Triangle' area of Birmingham at its peak, which is now a tourist attraction as well as an eating venue. The area's current restaurant turnover is estimated at a figure well in excess of £7m. It is easy to see how vital 'balti' is to the area in terms of employment and support of local suppliers - a typical balti house can use 2,000lbs of cooking onions and 300lbs of chicken breast in a week! Many staff work and live locally, their spending power also adding to the local economy.

Al Frash Balti - one of the balti restaurants in Birmingham's Balti Triangle.

Balti owes its introduction to Birmingham's large Pakistani and Kashmiri communities, who brought it to Birmingham through café-style restaurants, (the curry equivalent of transport cafes). It seemed to be that it was this simplicity that made the balti so popular. It didn't matter that there was no alcohol, none of the devout Muslim restaurant owners of the area had ever served that, anyway. It didn't matter that there were no

64

tablecloths and, in most cases, no cutlery. It didn't even matter that the food was basically a sauce. It was cheap and tasty, and it didn't take up too much of your drinking money. That was balti. The white population of the area loved it. Adopting and fiercely defending 'their' balti house, the phenomenon spreading like wildfire, turning even the most lucid and respectable businessman into a wide eyed fanatic.

It seemed that all our Birmingham-based business contacts at the time had a favourite whose virtues we should extol! Many a contract must have been cemented by a fearful supplicant singing the praises of a chewy balti lamb, scooped up with a fragment of hot fluffy, duvet-sized bread.

The balti craze spread rapidly in the 1990's and authors such as Pat Chapman and Mridula Baljekar produced whole books with 'authentic' recipes. Restaurateurs in other areas, who did not really understand what the cooking style was meant to be, but wanted to get in on the act, renamed their restaurants 'Balti House' and put the word balti in front of all the dishes they had been producing before. Newspapers wrote articles, television programmes hailed the new style, and Birmingham became the centre of the curry scene. Balti dining was fun. It might not have been stylish, but you could take your own booze and wine and dine for a pittance.

However, as the century faded so did the peak demand for balti. Balti Houses began to be squeezed by rising costs, but were trapped by their own marketing ploy, and could not raise prices to customers - it was, after all, a cheap and cheerful night out.

Today Birmingham remains the centre of balti cooking, and the Balti Triangle is still alive and well, although a little trimmed down. Several restaurants have changed their names back to tandoori, and many so-called baltis outside the West Midlands serving a variety of product that no Brummy balti aficionado would recognise.

The upmarket trend

Balti may have been the buzzword during the 1980s and 1990s at the economy end of the market, but, at the other end, was an element of the industry determined to break the glass ceiling and push the image of the Indian restaurant up into the dizzying heights of 'Haute Cuisine'.

The upward process had already been started by Amin Ali. His first attempt at elevating the Indian restaurant image *Jamdani*, was an enterprise in Wembley, which was either well before its time or the victim of poor location. His second, however, was an

Amin Ali of Red Fort

location. His second, however, was an entirely different story, and his *Red Fort* in Soho's Dean Street, opened in 1983 soon became the favourite of the smart set, attracting celebrities and politicians in their droves.

A year earlier, however, in 1982, Taj International Hotels flew in the face of advice and opened *The Bombay Brasserie* in Courtfield Road SW7 under Adi Modi, and successfully changed the entire Indian restaurant scene once again. The directors were told that the British would never be interested in the authentic cuisine of Bombay. They would not understand it and who had ever heard of Parsee food, for example? Neither would they pay the more expensive prices, the detractors said. The name, too, came under attack. Indian restaurants were called things like The Star of India or Nawab.

Above & below : London's Bombay Brasserie

Intriguingly enough, one of the main critics of the name was the Chairman of Taj, the late J.R. Tata, who felt that the word *Brasserie* was 'inappropriate for a top-class Indian restaurant'. Camellia Panjabi, the strong-minded young woman in his employ, whose idea all this had been, stuck to her guns, and the spacious breakfast room at the Bailey's Hotel in Gloucester Road, was converted into a grand Raj-style *Gymkhana*. (No, not a sandy area where young ladies, called Tamara and Sophie, trot around on fat-bellied Thelwell cartoon ponies). The word Gymkhana means 'ball-house', and only at the height of the Raj did it transfer to being synonymous with sports' clubhouses and thence to the Pony Club circuit.

Not only was everyone talking about The Bombay Brasserie, it soon became the benchmark for the industry.

Finally, after a Bombay astrologer, Mr Sohoni, was consulted to decide upon an auspicious date for the launch, the Bombay Brasserie was opened on December 10th 1982. The cynics soon found themselves eating humble korma. No-one sums it up better than Ismail Merchant, Indian film producer and director, writing in his foreword to *The Bombay Brasserie Cookbook* (Udit Sarkhel, Pavilion Books Ltd 1996). *"When The Bombay Brasserie opened in 1982 I was out of the country and therefore unable to accept the invitation to its inauguration: by the time I returned it seemed that everyone in London was talking about it. As a native of Bombay and a passionate cook I was curious to know what all the fuss was about, went there with some friends, and was immediately impressed by its cool, colonial style, by the efficiency of the staff and, above all, by the food."* Not only was everyone talking about The Bombay Brasserie, it soon became the benchmark for the Industry. Suddenly everyone saw the possibilities: Indian food could not only be presented in a more authentic way it could be presented in a more up-market way, too.

Style complements top class food at Iqbal Wahhab's Cinnamon Club

Most of the previous owners and chefs in the industry had learned their trade 'hands on,' but now a new dimension had been added with the coming of the highly professional Taj Group into the scene. A new class of chef was to appear, a chef able to cross all cultural divides, backed by years of classical, (including European basic), training in Taj and Oberoi management colleges.

Others follow suit

Soon London boasted several top-class establishments such as Namita Panjabi's *Chutney Mary*, Amin Ali's *The Red Fort, Tamarind, La Port des Indes, Cafe Lazeez*, Cyrus Todiwala's *Cafe Spice Namaste, Chor Bizarre*, Andy Varma's *Vama The Indian Room,* and more recently, *Zaika, Quilon* and Iqbal Wahhab's *Cinnamon Club*. Enam Ali of *Le Raj* in Epsom, Winner of the International Indian Chef of the Year in 1992/93, set a new standard for Bangladeshi restaurants, becoming one of the founder members of *The Guild of Bangladeshi Restaurateurs*, created to serve their community alongside the older *Bangladesh Caterers Association*, first started in 1960.

Two Indian restaurants - *Tamarind* and *Zaika* in London - were soon to be recognised by the culinary establishment with a Michelin star apiece and the Indian restaurant had finally come of age, completing the transition from dockside curry to food of the stars. The glass ceiling was not only broken - it had been shattered!

The first modern curry houses in 1960 numbered just 500. 1970 had seen this grow to 1,200. With the influx after Bangladesh Independence numbers grew rapidly to 3,000 in 1980. By 2,000 there were almost 8,000 Indian restaurants in Britain, turning over more than £2 billion a year, and employing some 70,000 people - one of the major industries in the country - but always under-rated. The new millennium changed all that, however, with the acceptance by the mainstream establishment, in the form of Michelin, the sector had entered the Premiership!

Two Indian restaurants were soon recognised by Michelin

Other ethnic restaurants have risen to challenge the Indian sector, but only the Chinese have made any real inroads to date. The first wave of Chinese immigrants, who arrived in the second half of the 19th Century, came after China's defeat in the Opium Wars and, as with the lascars, were mainly seamen. They jumped ship in Britain and settled in the port cities of Liverpool, Cardiff and London and as the new century dawned, the movement away from the docks to the cities, into first laundries, then catering, began. The earliest arrivals were also often associated with the East India Company and settled in the East End in general, and Limehouse in particular, by the 1880's.

Chung Koon, a former ship's chef on the Red Funnel Line, who had settled in London and married an English girl, was a pivotal figure in the sector. Koon opened the very smart *Maxim's* in Soho in 1908 and soon after, *The Cathay* in Glasshouse Street, which became a Japanese establishment in 1996

By 1913 there were thirty shops and cafés for Chinese people in Pennyfield and Limehouse Causeway, although this 'mini boom' was to decline rapidly by the 1930's as shipping slumped.

By the 1950's the Chinese community began to focus on Soho in London because of the theatre trade, and when diplomatic relations standardised in 1950, several Mandarin speaking former diplomats opened Peking-style restaurants.

General de Gaulle had to seek out The Cathay to get away from an Anglo-Saxon diet he despised.

This movement continued and by the 1960's Soho had become London's Chinatown. The flow outward to the suburbs and elsewhere started, in much the same way as in the Indian sector.

Even though, there were fewer than 5,000 Chinese in Britain up until the War and it was not until after the Second World War that Chinese food gained any real popularity, chiefly fostered by American servicemen taking English girls to *The Cathay*. This trend, in turn, was supported by returning British servicemen with a taste for Oriental food acquired during overseas postings. It is said that even General de Gaulle had to seek out The Cathay to get away from an Anglo-Saxon diet he despised.

Chung Koon's son, John, was born in 1926 and took over *The Cathay* in 1957. He opened the first real up-market Chinese restaurant, *Lotus House* in 1958. Such was the demand for his food that John Koon then did the un-heard of, and launched the first ever Chinese takeaway in London's Queensway, and followed it up by convincing Billy Butlin to open a Chinese kitchen in every Butlins Holiday Camp with a simple menu of Chicken Chop Suey and Chips. The Chinese quickly adopted the takeaway principle, (as well as capitalising on the British love for fish and chips), and soon most small villages and towns had their Chinese takeaway, which doubled as a fish and chip shop. Despite the continued growth of Thai and even Japanese restaurants, Chinese establishments have presented the only real threat to the continued growth of the Indian sector to the present day.

Throughout the second half of the 20th century the Indian restaurant industry went from an insignificant eating-out venue for the lads after a few pints to the 9000 strong restaurant sector we know today. The extra charge for 'on or off the bone' or 'white meat', which was common in those early days, has disappeared as quality and standards have grown immeasurably.

The war years of the twentieth century completely reversed natural cuisine development, with many on an almost starvation diet and most meals bulked-out to compensate for lack of meat and dairy produce. Few exotic foods or spices were available in Europe and vegetables predominated with bread, tea and potatoes.

J. Lyons & Co Ltd opened their first establishment in Coventry Street in 1907 and the Strand in London in 1912. Such was the success of their simple concept (cheap,cheerful, fast and vaste) that *Maison Lyons* was opened near Marble Arch in 1933, seating 2,000 people and employing 1,000 staff, but even at that it did not equal the 4,000 seating at Coventry Street.

The cream of Britain's and Europe's men had been lost in the 1914-18 war and the Great Depression of the 'twenties added to the misery, but the Empire Exhibition at Wembley in 1924 put on a brave imperial face and did much to legitimise ethnic foods. The exhibition boasted a Mughal palace (operated by Edward Palmer, the man who went on to open Veeraswamy's in London), a Nigerian fortress, a Hong Kong street and even a Samoan house.

The beginning of the Second World War put Britain back to subsistence eating, with food rationing for bacon, ham, butter, sugar, cooking fat, meat, tea, cheese, jam, eggs and sweets being introduced in 1940. Lemons and oranges disappeared overnight and luxury fruits were sold at amazing prices. Bananas also disappeared as did, strangely, onions, and in 1941 melons were selling at £2 each, a staggering £68.32 when converted to today's values! Then, just when people thought the hardships were over, bread rationing was introduced in 1946 and remained until 1948. However, the Second World War did introduce an enforced understanding of the need for a nutritionally balanced diet, however shortlived.

Lyons Corner House

The post war years gradually saw the return to restaurant dining, with groups like *Berni* (the first one opening in Bristol selling steak, chips and peas) and *Beefeater,* and a gradual international influence in the foods eaten in Britain. *The Good Food Guide* was established and Elizabeth David wrote her famous '*Book of Mediterranean Food & French Country Cooking*', which set multitudes of middle-class housewives trundling off in search of such exotic ingredients as olive oil. The first chain of burger bars in Britain, *Wimpy* opened in 1954 and by 1956 Britain boasted 3,000 self-service stores, as food shopping started to change in style.

In the mid-fifties the package tour began to show itself, becoming the accepted form of overseas holiday over the following ten years, and the process of British people learning overseas cuisines at first hand began. Immigration became an important factor in the development of cuisine as peoples from British interests all over the world arrived seeking a new life and bringing their culture and cuisines. Political changes in India, with Partition into India and East & West Pakistan, on August 15th 1947, causing great upheaval, as did the Independence of East Pakistan, (originally East Bengal), on 26th March 1971, to become Bangladesh. Between 1951 and 1961 the number of Pakistanis in Britain grew from 5,000 to 24,000 - Indians from 38,800 to 81,400 - West Indians from 25,300 to 171,800 - East Asians from 12,000 to 29,600 and West African from 5,600 to 19,800.

Peoples from old British colonies all over the world arrived in the country bringing with them their cultures and cuisines.

Fast food appeared, with *Pizza Express* starting up in 1965, although *McDonalds* were relative latecomers, only appearing in 1974, and the 1960's saw a veritable feast of new food styles, with ethnic food becoming very popular in some sections of the community.

By 1966 the retail emphasis had moved from the self-service store to the supermarket with 2,500 outlets available to the British public, reflecting the swing towards speed and convenience.

In the nineteen-sixties you could buy a good meal out for under £1 (£11.26 at modern day values) and a bottle of wine for 15 shillings (£8.44), whilst the posh restaurants catered to the expense account, until Chancellor of the Exchequer James Callaghan closed the tax loophole. Chains such as *Berni Inns* and *Forte* mushroomed everywhere. The British had found a pastime they enjoyed even if they weren't too adventurous at this early stage: a typical meal consisted of tomato soup or prawn cocktail, followed by roast meat and two veg, finished off with Peach Melba or trifle.

Wherever groups of immigrants were to be found restaurants sprang up offering exotic foods such as moussaka, kebabs, goulash and paella.

Meanwhile the impact of the immigrant community was having an effect. Wherever groups of immigrants were to be found, restaurants sprang up offering exotic foods such as moussaka, kebabs, goulash and paella. Chinese restaurants spread apace, outstripping the gradually blooming

Indian sector for a while, with real Cantonese food being re-interpreted for the British palate as sweet and sour pork and Chop Suey, actually an American import, the dish having first appeared in its modern form in San Francisco at the end of the 19th century. Apparently only the name has any links with China, *tsap seui* being Cantonese for 'mixed scraps'.

Fast and cheap

Curry houses, being both economical and tolerant of youthful horseplay, became the places to go for the student set, and all university towns boasted a good selection. In Cambridge, the curry houses were the place to go for undergraduates, with the more macho males competing with each other to consume hotter and hotter curries, much to the amusement of their vendors. By 1966 The Good Food Guide included recommendations for a Polish restaurant in Glasgow, a Chinese cafe in Liverpool and a Shish Kebab in Manchester.

The tandoor made meals even faster

Curry houses in the sixties did not have the reputation of being purveyors of fine food and were seen by many as rather strange places run by mysterious people. Unfortunately tolerance was not a strong feature of the time amongst some parts of the white sector of the community, and the treatment of many Indian waiters was often atrocious.

The owners and staff of Indian restaurants - particularly the staff - worked long hours to please their customers, and no service was too much, despite the fact that customer and waiter could often not understand each other.

Owners looked at the successful British restaurants of the time, *Beefeater*, *Aberdeen Angus Steakhouses* and *Berni*, and copied their style of decor - red-flocked wallpaper and red velour seating. They looked at the successful Chinese restaurants, the way they filled their menus with endless lists of dishes, and produced extensive menus of their own.

A group of lads coming in after closing time were not prepared to wait long for their food

The problem was that Indian restaurant food in Britain had to be cheap, but the level of knowledge in the kitchen was reasonably basic. The only answer was to create a style of cooking that encompassed the extensive menu concept and yet which could be produced economically and speedily - a group of 'lads' coming in after the pubs closed were not prepared to wait long for their food. The answer was the 'one pot masala' adopted by much of the Bengali sector, which, known today as Bangladeshi restaurants, accounts for well over half of all 'Indian' restaurants in Britain. The untrained chef produced a basic gravy or masala; a basic, mild sauce, usually consisting of onions, ginger, garlic and tomato puree, which brewed hour after hour in big pots on the oven ranges. He then waited for the order of Madras, Vindaloo or Korma and added one or two spoons of chilli powder to vary the heat, colouring to vary the colour, and perhaps yoghurt or cream to vary the consistency. Thus the basic British Indian menu was born to cater for the perceived requirements of the British customer. The formula for the successful curry house was established: a wide choice; 'themed' surroundings; servile staff, and meals on the table in a matter of minutes to cater for the impatient and sometimes abusive customer.

Then the tandoor arrived and made a fast operation even faster, enabling chefs to produce the wonderful breads that became so popular. It was a fast and very tasty method of cooking and did not need great expertise, except to avoid the third degree burns that every tandoor novice acquires on his forearm.

Most restaurateurs in the sector were not caterers by training or inclination and communication was always difficult, with levels of illiteracy high amongst many of the immigrant communities.

Chefs learned their basic skills in one Indian restaurant then opened their own elsewhere.

Despite these disadvantages, they had a natural commercial cunning and an almost instinctive marketing ability, and realised that continued peace, international travel and a growing *laissez faire* attitude amongst British people at the birth of the 'Permissive Society', offered an opportunity they could thrive in. Indian restaurants were not popular at home (Indians rarely ate Indian food out, although, when they did, Chinese food was preferred), and 'curry', of course, was unknown.

Gradually British Indian cuisine developed to reflect British tastes. Added to this, of course, was the fact that, because people who had learned their basic skills in another Indian restaurant elsewhere in Britain were opening new restaurants, they retained a similar menu and style. This 'if it ain't broke don't fix it!' policy was probably the basis on which the industry was built. Consequently, as restaurants grew in a seemingly geometric progression, the product offered remained roughly the same, and it actually gave the appearance of a standard, authentic cuisine - which was hugely enjoyed in Britain, but scarcely recognisable to visitors from India and the rest of the subcontinent.

The Kashmir - the oldest established curry restaurant in Bradford

British Indian cuisine developed to reflect British tastes.

When immigration surged again after Bangladeshi Independence in 1971, it brought with it extended families living in local communities, providing a ready labour force with which to operate old and new restaurants alike.

The nation's favourite dish

In the mid sixties the now famous Chicken Tikka Masala appeared, specifically created to cater to the sweet, gravy-loving British taste. The British curry-loving public took the new offering to their hearts, and has been exported around the world including India.

The flagship dish of Britain's newly acclaimed 'national cuisine,' boasts a huge 15% of the sales of the almost half a million curries consumed, on average, in the restaurants and homes of the United Kingdom every day of the year.

Chicken Tikka Masala, or CTM as it was affectionately dubbed by Colleen in '*Spice 'n Easy Magazine*' in November 1994, is one of those culinary fables that lend a touch of intrigue and excitement to an already exotic cuisine, and, with its exact origins virtually untraceable, its success remains an enigma.

The interest in CTM is quite unbelievable, and we estimate that it forms the subject of well over 60% of all enquiries directed at us from the media, both in Britain and internationally.

In an article in The Daily Telegraph in November 1999, journalist Amit Roy referred to it as a dish that does not exist in Indian cuisine. So the question is, 'is it a genuine Indian dish or isn't it?'

Amit Roy was quite correct to observe that the dish does not hail from India, and that it was specifically created to appeal to the British palate by some very astute restaurateurs. This much is not in doubt, but when one moves on to trace the history of the dish, fact blurs into fiction and its story differs depending on just who one talks to.

It all started with tikka (seen below) and then came the masala part so that soon CTM was being enjoyed all over Britain in all shades from glowing red to gentle green.

Chicken Tikka Masala

In 2002, the Best in Britain Awards (BIBA), held a competition to find the 'Chicken Tikka Masala of the Year'. The winning recipe came from *Manzoor Ahmed*, chef and co-owner of the *Tabaq* in South Clapham, London.

Manzoor's CTM

CTM is made in two stages. Firstly the chicken must be marinated and cooked; then a sauce must be prepared for them to be served in.

Marinade:

Ingredients

1lb	large diced boneless chicken breast		
1oz	garlic	1 oz	ginger
4 tbs	fresh natural yoghurt	2	small fresh green chillies
1 tbs lemon juice		1 tsp	salt
1 tsp	zeera (cumin) powder	1 tsp	dhanya (coriander) powder
1 tbs red paprika		4-5 leaves fresh green coriander	

Method:

Grind fresh green chillies, fresh coriander, garlic and ginger with 2-3 tbs of water, until a thick paste is formed. Marinate chicken in the paste, then add the salt and the yoghurt to the mixture. Next add the lemon juice, zeera powder, dhanya powder and red paprika, and mix the chicken and other ingredients thoroughly. Leave the chicken to marinate in the paste overnight.

Manzoor Ahmed

SAUCE

Ingredients:

4 oz	chopped onions	3oz ghee
1 oz	garlic (ground)	4 oz fresh single cream
1oz	ginger (ground)	2 medium tomatoes (liquidised)
3oz	yoghurt -	½ tsp salt - ¼ tsp chilli powder
½ tsp	zeera powder	½ tsp dhanya powder
2 lbs	desiccated coconut	pinch dried methi (fenugreek leaves)

Method:

Take previously marinated chicken and cook on skewers in tandoor. If this is not possible, leave chicken for 10-12 minutes under a grill on a moderate high heat.

Meanwhile the sauce can be prepared:
Fry the onions in the ghee until lightly brown. Add tomatoes and yoghurt to the onions and mix on a low/moderate heat. Next, add the zeera powder, chilli powder, dhanya powder, salt, desiccated coconut, dried methi and fresh single cream to the mixture and mix thoroughly. Water may be added if a more liquid sauce is desired. Add cooked pieces of chicken to the sauce and mix in well. Leave to simmer on a low heat.
To finish, transfer the completed CTM to a serving dish and garnish by pouring a small quantity of single cream over the dish and then sprinkle liberally with fresh coriander and garam masala.

Chicken Tikka Masala does not come from the Raj, or the kitchens of the Moghul Emperors, but millions of people enjoy it every year and perhaps that is all the pedigree it needs!

Top restaurateur Amin Ali recalls serving CTM when he first arrived in London in 1974

No 'Indian' chef seems to have produced any real evidence that he or she first invented the dish, and it is commonly thought that its invention came about almost by accident. Journalist and restaurateur Iqbal Wahhab claims it was created when a Bangladeshi chef produced a dish of traditional Chicken Tikka, only to be asked, where's my gravy? The response was, supposedly, a can of Campbell's cream of tomato soup and a few spices and the 'masala' element was born. Top food writer Charles Campion refers to CTM as a dish invented in London in the Seventies so that the ignorant could have gravy with their chicken tikka. Several chefs have laid claim to the invention of CTM, but none with any concrete evidence or witness support, so a mystery it will have to remain.

The descendants of Sultan Ahmed Ansari, who owned the *Taj Mahal* in Glasgow claim he invented it in the 1950s, but there is no other evidence of the dish at this early date or of the tandoor, necessary for the production of the main ingredient, chicken tikka, in Glasgow so early. Top restaurateur Amin Ali, owner of *The Red Fort* in London's Soho, recalls serving CTM when he first arrived in London in 1974. A lowly waiter at the time, he remembers wondering just what the dish was.

One family to have gained tangible benefits from the success of CTM is that of Sheik Abdul Khalique, who owns *The Polash* in Shoeburyness, Essex, which opened in 1979. His father, Haji Abdul Razzah, returned to Bangladesh in 1985, having made sufficient profit from a restaurant whose most popular dish was CTM, to build *The Polash Hotel* in Sylhet. A Mosque and The Polash Sheba Charitable Trust were added after his death. The family firmly claim their fortunes are largely down to CTM, the mysterious

The Polash, Shoeburyness on its Silver Jubilee

Indian/British hybrid. CTM was introduced to the supermarket chill cabinets, via Waitrose, by G.K.Noon in 1983, when he himself was still in the United States. The stage was set, and by the end of the Millennium, it was generally acknowledged as the most popular single dish in Britain.

For something that is so popular with the public and with the restaurateurs who make their living from it, Chicken Tikka Masala is still very much the Cinderella of culinary creations. Very few recipes for CTM appear in the plethora of Indian Cuisine cookbooks that have appeared over the last twenty years, and Alan Davidson's recent tome, *Oxford Companion to Food,* regarded by serious 'foodies' as the definitive reference work, does not even consider it deserving of a listing.

Indeed, such are the passions it generates in the industry, that many top chefs refuse to cook or serve it due to its complete 'lack of authenticity'

Although CTM may have been created on the spur of the moment, as a culinary concept, the dish already existed

However, exist it does and demanded it is, so just what is Chicken Tikka Masala?

Tikkas are the bite-sized chunks you cut the chicken into, and these are marinated and then cooked in the tandoor, the hot clay oven, which sears the outside of the meat to browned crispness; the quick cooking method retaining a moist succulence inside.

The masala part is where things become most difficult. Masala means spices, but no exact recipe or formula for these seems to exist. CTM can be yellow, red, brownish or even green, and can be very creamy, a little creamy, chilli-hot or quite mild. In restaurants it tends to be a creamy sauce - not too hot; a bit tomatoey; very smooth and, all too often, quite sweet and very red. In supermarkets, once you have by-passed the masses of CTM sandwiches, pizzas, filled pancakes, kievs, pies, microwave rolls, wraps and so on, you come to the chilled and frozen ready meals, which range from a mild onion gravy, to saffron cream to velvety vermilion. Created on the spur of the moment under pressure it may have been but as a culinary concept, the dish, if not the name, already existed. The North Indian dishes, *Murg Masallum* and *Murgh Makhani* have been part of the traditional Indian cook's repertoire for many years. *The Bombay Palace Cookbook* by Stendahl in 1985 listed a recipe for *Palace Murgh Kari*, incorporating yoghurt, tomato paste and heavy cream, and Niru Gupta's *'Everyday Indian'* (1995) lists *Murgh Rasedar*, which includes most of the required ingredients, including cream, tomatoes and onions.

The shape of things to come may have been a recipe for *Shahi Chicken Masala* in Mrs Balbir Singh's '*Indian Cookery*' published in 1961(the recipe was not included until the 1975 edition); one of the earliest Indian cookery books written by an Indian and aimed at the English speaking population. Such seemed to be the book's popularity that, in its first 10 years, the volume went to six reprints.

Mridula Baljekar is one of the few cookery writers to have included CTM in her bestselling '*Complete Indian Cookbook*' (1993), including food colouring and tomato puree in her version, as well as double cream and almonds. Chef, Mohammed Moneer introduces yet another ingredient, substituting half a cup of coconut milk for the cream.

It seems that the ingredients generally include yoghurt, tomatoes, cream and spices, as well as the chicken pieces, and if you have been lucky enough to find a version that suits you then stick to it. The *Spice 'n Easy* article in 1993 endeavoured to produce the definitive recipe from forty eight versions on offer and came up with a 'standard' version basically a composite of all the recipes polled for the article. However, we have tracked down a more recent, award-winning recipe for you. (See feature on pages 86-87)

The KISS principle

The British have always been club orientated and, as curry fans began to identify with the dishes placed before them in Indian restaurants, the club concept came into full play.

Based on the KISS principle (keep it simple stupid), restaurateurs organised their sixties and seventies menus into four simple categories - mild, medium, hot and help!

Korma became, (incorrectly), known as the mildest of mild dishes, rich in cream or yoghurt, nuts and saffron and the obvious choice of curry virgins. The next step up was Chicken Tikka, Tandoori Chicken or Chicken Tikka Masala - a little spicy, but sweet from added sugar, and nothing in there to keep you up all night. The next rung on the heat ladder took you into the realms of being a full club member; strong enough and knowledgeable enough to go for Meat Madras - another dish made up by an opportunist chef facing demands for a hotter curry, having nothing to do with the city itself, where it was unknown.

Rich & mild Chicken Korma

By now you had reached a chilli heat that would make your scalp tingle.

The vindaloo was mouth-seeringly, mind-numbingly hot

However, the peak of achievement of the 'eight pints then go for a curry lads', became the vindaloo, bindaloo or even tindaloo (these latter two seem to have been the creation of either an over-fertile imagination, or someone bent on suicide). Once again, a dish incorrectly interpreted as mouth-seeringly, mind numbingly hot, and which demanded further copious pints of lager and much untoward behaviour - as well as the by now obligatory uncomfortable experience the following morning. Enough, you would think? No, there was a certain masochistic element, who could not stop there. Suddenly, from nowhere, appeared the *phal*, the quasi 'Indian' dish that was to become the ultimate expression of British manhood.

92

Dum Biryani at Cafe Lazeez, Soho

Byriani is not a spicy hot dish at all

Even whiz-kid advertising copywriters knew very little about this exotic cuisine that seemed to be creating a buzz, especially amongst the young. Carling Black Label Lager produced a TV advert in the 1970s with the strap line, 'that will cool your biryani down a bit', and it did not even occur to watching millions at the time that a biryani is not a spicy hot dish at all! Even then, people were not too sure. The hangover from the early sixties had left many wondering just what went into these spicy dishes, and rumours about stray cats and other stomach-churning possibilities were rife. It is probably for this reason that those wanting to venture forth tended to go for chicken, easily identified.

The crafty restaurateurs, undaunted by any implied insult, took advantage by introducing the 'on or off the bone syndrome' and charged extra for those wanting white meat.

It has only been with the publishing of numerous Indian cookery books and the move upmarket, that people have cared that korma is actually a cooking style (braised).

The basic menu was to remain the same until the mid-eighties and this still represents the backbone of the industry today. It has only been with the publishing of numerous Indian cookbooks and the move up-market, that people have cared that *korma* is actually a cooking style (braised) and can be mild or hot; *dopiaza*, though rich with onions, probably does not mean 'twice onions' but reflects the name of Mogul creator, Mullah Dopiaza; *rogon josh* has to be lamb - but who cares - why not *chicken* rogon josh?; *jhalfrezi* means stir-fried with spices, with no reference to the normal mouth-numbing heat; *vindaloo* is a Portguese dish, derived from their words, *vi ñho* (vinegar) and (*alio*) garlic and can be hot or not; and *dhansak*, the famous Parsi dish, does not normally include aubergines, pineapple, peaches or even apricots, and should strictly be a lamb dish - even though *chicken* dhansak is one of the most popular dishes in Britain.

The Indian menu remained unchallenged until the eighties when the *balti* reared its head in Birmingham. *Karahi* cooking had long been part of the Indian repertoire, but suddenly the same style re-appeared on the streets of Ladypool Road and Stratford Road under the name of balti, complete with its own legends and fanatics.

Specialist supplies

The continuing growth in the popularity of Indian cuisine was certain to attract specialist suppliers to offer the ingredients needed in the restaurants.
In 1956 L.K.Pathak (1925-1997) arrived in Britain from Kenya, and began to supply products to the then infant industry from a shop in Drummond Street, London. In 1962 he started a small factory and the *Patak* brand was born. In 1976 son Kirit met and married Meena, a talented cook, who was to be responsible for the development of many of the sauces and products produced by the company. In 1978 the family

Patak's has been one of the major players in bringing Indian food to the general public

moved from London to Wigan and the company grew rapidly. Ranges of sauces and chutneys were aimed initially at the restaurants, and then home-use products began to appear in order to meet the new, consumer-led, demand from the supermarkets. By the end of the 20th century Pataks products were in markets all over the world, and Kirit and Meena stood high in the ranks of Britain's richest Asians.

Iqbal Ahmed arrived in Manchester from Bangladesh in 1971, and also saw the possibilities in the ethnic food sector. By 1980 he had a purpose-built cold store, created for his seafood range, and he began exporting his and his brother's brand, *Mr Prawn*, *Tiger*, *Seagold* and other goods in 1992 through their company, Seafood Marketing International. Today they have a turnover in the region of £70 million.

In 1956, LK Pathak arrived in Britain from Kenya, and began to supply products from a shop in Drummond Street, London NW1

Rice is a basic requirement of the Indian food industry in Britain, and specialists were quick to recognise the niche market.

In 1972 Rashmi Thrakrar was expelled from Uganda, then under the Idi 'Dada' Amin dictatorship, and set up in Harrow providing Basmati for the Asian community. In 1978 his operation moved to the Midlands and then in 1988 to Europe's largest rice mill in Rainham, Essex. Nowadays *Tilda Rice* sells to 40 countries around the world. By contrast Moni Varma had been a successful businessman in Malawi when he moved to London with wife Shoba in 1981 and started *Veetee Rice*. In 1992 the company opened its base in Rochester, Kent and is now one of the major rice suppliers in Britain and internationally.

The supermarkets were quite slow to recognise the growth in popularity of Indian cuisine. In the 1980s several of

Sir Gulam K. Noon MBE at Bombay Brasserie watched by
General Manager Adi Modi.

97

the major players dipped their toe into the water with rather inferior products, but soon it hit home that here was a true marketing phenomenon.

Soon Tesco, Sainsbury, and Asda were cautiously offering cooking sauces in the Indian style, followed rapidly by chilled and frozen products. Each company looked around for the best companies to produce these specialist items for them, creating a great opportunity for those equipped to take advantage.

The only company known for producing ethnic products at the turn of the nineteenth century was *J.A. Sharwood* founded in 1889. In 1964 Sharwoods was bought by Cerebos and in 1971 Tiffany Sharwood was set up to produce frozen products. In 1986 first Tiffany's then Sharwoods was purchased by RHM and the group continued its growth in Indian as well as other ethnic foods.

Soon Sainsbury's and Waitrose recognised the excellence of Noon products and the company started production for these two major supermarkets

G.K.Noon was born into the *Royal Sweet* family in India and arrived in Britain in 1973 to set up business. In 1988 a factory was built in Southall and Birds Eye became the first major contract. Soon Sainsbury and Waitrose recognised the excellence of the Noon products and production for those two major supermarkets commenced. In 1993 the *Noon* brand was created, then a factory fire in 1994 caused a temporary setback. But it was to be short-lived. In 1998 Noon products was sold to WT Foods for £58.1 million and Sir Gulam Noon MBE later became President of the London Chamber of Commerce.

One of the fastest stories of success in any industry was that of Perween Warsi and her husband Talib, who came from India in 1974 and settled in Derby. Perween produced Indian foods from her kitchen until she set up S&A Foods in 1986, named after her sons Sadiq and Abid. By 1987 the company was producing Indian products for ASDA and Safeway and went from strength to strength, expanding its product base into other ethnic cuisines, such as Mexican and Thai, with Perween becoming one of the most successful Asian women in Britain.

Gradually supermarket products ranged from curry crisps to chicken tikka masala pizza as the demand for all foods associated with the sub-continent

Companies such as Geeta Samtani's 'Geeta's Foods' and Nighat Ahwan's 'Shere Khan' began producing quality sauces, chutneys and pastes.

grew. Balti was absorbed rapidly into the overall culture, zooming to a fantastic peak of popularity, then settling down to become just tenth in the popularity list of dishes ordered in restaurants today.

When the Indian restaurant came to Britain they were all indeed, truly Indian, but things changed after 1947 and again after 1971 redefining and re-categorising them into Indian, Pakistani and Bangladeshi - not to forget Sri Lankan and Nepalese. Although each of these sectors is anxious not to lose its cultural heritage, it was soon realised that the British were happier calling it all just 'Indian' as it has always been and thus things stayed until 1982 and the arrival of *The Bombay Brasserie* in London. This did not just ring the changes in menu terms - with not a sign of Chicken Tikka Masala or Meat Madras anywhere - but more fundamentally, in standard terms, taking Indian restaurants up-market, which only restaurants such as *Veeraswamy* or Amin Ali's *Red Fort* had previously attempted to do.

Chutney Mary, with its then unique Anglo-Indian style, opened and a new breed of chef appeared in Britain.

A few years later *Chutney Mary,* with its then unique Anglo-Indian style, opened and a new breed of chef appeared in Britain. Not for these restaurants a kitchen brigade self-taught through hands-on experience, but rather highly-qualified graduates of managerial and catering colleges in India with, experience in five-star hotel groups such as Taj, Oberoi and Sheraton, who had cut their teeth cooking for celebrities and heads of state.

By the mid-nineties there was an obvious split between the style of British Indian restaurant and the cuisine that had been successful for over 40 years and the newer, regional style of Indian cuisine, introducing dishes from the sub-continent's vast pantheon that had previously not seen the light of day on British shores.

The progress and development of the industry over the past fifty years or so has been truly amazing, such that curry has been declared the favourite British food, and Chicken Tikka Masala a British national dish. The formula of historical connections, immigration for labour force and unique British demand for the exotic and spicy harking back to days of yore, had worked their magic and created something unique in the world and very strange to many outsiders.

So why do people keep going back for more?

Why do normally sane people sudden suffer cravings for a curry when they might be thousands of miles away from their own local haunt?

We've actually met people, basking in the Florida sun by the side of the pool at a five star hotel, who have paused in the serious task of skin-burning, to enquire whether we know their particular favourite restaurant, after first declaring, "I'd kill for a good curry!"

Hot, hot, hot

The secret is all in the addictive nature of the chilli pepper used in modern curries(see feature on pages 104-105), and it has us coming back for more and more. It doesn't even matter what type of chilli used, either. There are more than 1,600 varieties of this little plant, whose relatives include the tomato, the potato and deadly nightshade. Two hundred of these are grown in Mexico alone.

Capsaicin is an alkaloid that causes the heat in all varieties of peppers, and is the magic ingredient, both for the 'bite' and medicinally. This is found in its largest concentrations in the white placental central core that holds the seeds and in the seeds themselves. It encourages the flow of gastric juices, which is why some people find their mouths water at the mere mention of chilli, and promotes regular peristalsis movement, (the reflex action of the

gut on food, which moves it through the digestive system), further aiding digestion and preventing flatulence.

The heat of the chilli can be affected by the climate and soil it is grown in and by its ripeness when eaten.

Scientists have managed to find five capsaicinoid components, three of which give a 'rapid bite' and two a long, low intensity on tongue and mid-palate, the ratios of which vary from type to type and account for the differences in pungency and 'burn' sensation.

One of the other components of chilli, *capsidicin*, is a natural antibiotic, and it has been found to possess antibacterial and anti-fungal properties, and has been used since ancient times as a powerful pain killer: Capsaicin ointment is available to help relieve arthritis and inflamed joints.

103

Chilli

One of the items on the shopping list for Columbus' trip in 1492, on which he accidentally discovered the Americas, had been the 'King of Spices', pepper. Imagine his delight when one of the plants he discovered actually produced a pepper, albeit a strange variety. It almost made up for the fact that he had slipped up in not finding an alternative route to the spice-rich East Indies.

The 'new' pepper he had discovered in the 'New World', was *capsicum frutescens*, the chilli pepper. They weren't 'new' over there, however; Native Americans had been using them,

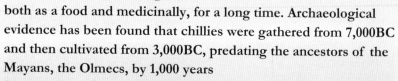

both as a food and medicinally, for a long time. Archaeological evidence has been found that chillies were gathered from 7,000BC and then cultivated from 3,000BC, predating the ancestors of the Mayans, the Olmecs, by 1,000 years

Some suggest that the fact that its seeds are encased in a fleshy pod or capsule gave it its botanical genus name, capsicum. Others say that its root is from the Greek for 'I bite' - Kapto. Either explanation would seem to have its merits. The common names are easier to track down: Cayenne is named after the capital of French Guyana; chilli is an altered form of Chile, after the country - it is still spelt this way in the United States; and piment and pimento from the Spanish word for pepper, pimiento.

This fiery little fruit soon became a favourite of the Portuguese, and Vasco da Gama took it with him on his marathon trip to India in 1498.

The plant flourished and found favour in tropical India, and its cultivation and use travelled through China, especially in Hunan and Szechuan, to come back, full circle, via the Turks.

The pepper that found its way back, however, had been altered by cultivation in the cooler north; Paprika, or pimento, is a member of the smoother, milder *capsicum annuum* branch of the family, which also includes the bell pepper. The capsicum arrived in Hungary in 1699 and only became an indispensable ingredient in their Gulyas (goulash), in the 18th century.

Today, the chilli, is the most popular spice in the world. Used all over the Indian sub-continent, it is also popular in Southeast Asia, Hunan and Szechuan in China, Central America and the USA, where, usually in sauce form, it is central to the Creole, Cajun and Texan cuisines. In Europe, Portugal, Spain, especially the Basques, and the Italian regions of Abruzzi and Basilicata, all use chilli. European Gypsies, too, were fond of peppers and used them in their love charms, and could even have contributed to their distribution throughout the continent.

The fruits of the chilli, like caraway, cumin and dill were also seen in folklore to inspire fidelity, and it was believed that two red peppers, tied together and placed under the marital pillow, would prevent a partner straying.

Researchers at Harvard Medical School discovered that capsaicin carries
out its action by binding to a receptor - a protein that sits on the surface of
a neuron or nerve cell.

Ironically, it seems to be the very pain produced by the alkaloid that helps
to produce the pain-killing effect: Capsaicin stimulates certain nerve
endings to manufacture the chemical, Substance P, which transmits the
sensation of pain through the nervous system. Eventually the cells are
exhausted, temporarily blocking pain signals to the brain. During these
processes, the body's natural defence mechanism stimulates the release of
endorphins, (natural pain-killers and tranquillisers which give a similar
effect to that of opium-based drugs such as morphine), in the brain,
reinforcing, perhaps, the addictive effect, leading to chilli-based foods such
as curry playfully being referred to as 'sex on a plate'.

Drinking more water after a spicy mouthful simply spreads the burning.

It is not soluble in water and it's stinging pungency can only be countered
by *casein*, a protein found in milk and its by-products such as cheese and
yoghurt, which is why *lassi*, the Indian yoghurt-based drink, is such a good
foil to an Indian meal.

Capsaicin also has an affinity for fat, explaining why drinking more water
after a spicy mouthful simply spreads the burning, whereas absorbing the
spice with another food, such as a yoghurt-based *raita* or bread is more
effective.

The heat of the chilli can be affected by the climate and soil where it is
grown and by its ripeness and a test exists, to determine the level of heat in

a chilli, called the Scoville Scale (founded by German chemist Wilbur Scoville pre-1920's). As a guide, the hottest on the scale was the *haba ñero* (up to 500,000 units) until the *naga jolokia* or *Tezpur* was found recently in Assam (850,000 units), and the mildest is the large, sweet bell pepper (0 units). The popular *jalapeno* is about 5,000 units.

However, chilli is not just a pretty sting.

Nutritionally, it is high in vitamin A and a source of vitamins B1, B2, niacin, sodium, phosphorous, potassium, calcium, iron, magnesium and zinc and, by weight, capsicum peppers contain between 6 to 9 times the amount of vitamin C than a tomato.

In herbalist witchcraft, the essential oil extracted from cardamom is used for love and lust.

This is good news indeed in these carcinogen-phobic times, as both vitamins A and C are powerful antioxidants, believed to protect against various forms of cancer and cardiovascular disease. Other research has found that the chilli can also help combat heart attack and stroke, as it appears to extend blood coagulation time, preventing harmful blood clots, and that it may also help to cut tri-glycerides and decrease bad cholesterol levels, when used in conjunction with a diet low in saturated fats.

But it is not chilli alone that makes Indian cuisine so unique and habit forming to the palate if not the brain. Many of the other spices and ingredients have a long pharmaceutical, as well as culinary history.

Both the Ancient Greek and Roman cultures regarded *cumin* seeds as a symbol of miserliness and greed, and the first century Roman Emperor, Antoninus Pius, was nicknamed 'The Cumin' because of his parsimonious nature. Cumin, like all other herbs and spices, has been used throughout

Top: *A spice dabba*
second row : Garlic - cardamon - fenugreek
third row : Cumin - ginger
Bottom : Turmeric - saffron

history in the practice of folk magic, where it is used principally as an ingredient in incense when preparing for protection, exorcism of evil, fidelity and to combat theft. As with many of the other 'curry' spices, it does actually contain a combination of antioxidants that may be helpful in combating many of the 'modern' diseases, such as stroke, high blood pressure and cancers: Vitamin C and the carotenoid, vitamin A, which are powerful antioxidants; vitamin B1 (Thiamin), which helps in the proper metabolism of foods; minerals like potassium, which helps the body to regulate body fluids, heart rhythm, and aid in the maintenance of normal blood pressure rates.

The first recorded use of *cardamom* appears in Ayurvedic texts from around 4th century BC, mentioned as a cure for urinary tract infections and as a weight loss aid, and the ancient Greeks were already trading the spice by that time. In herbalist witchcraft, the essential oil of cardamom is used in magic for love and lust!

During the Middle Ages, *fenugreek* acquired something of a reputation as an aphrodisiac and was used by 'witches' and folk healers in love potions and as a cure for impotence. Modern chemical analysis has actually detected the presence of a substance, *diosgenin*, which acts in a similar way to the body's own sex hormones, so, whilst we don't have any actual personal experience as to its efficacy, perhaps they were actually on to something! *Unani Tibb*, the system of botanical medicine and dietetics developed by the Persian physician *Avicenna*, lists fenugreek as being an effective curative for coughs, tuberculosis, bronchitis, fevers, sore throat, neuralgia, sciatica, swollen glands, skin eruptions, wounds tumours, sores, asthma and emphysema.

Chinese texts from around 3000 BC described *garlic* as the healing plant, showing a long understanding of its benefits to health. The Egyptians are believed to have worshipped garlic and clay model bulbs were found in

Tutankhamun's tomb. The Ancient Greeks used it to treat gangrene and Hippocrates, the father of medicine, used garlic vapours to treat cervical cancers in around 300 BC. They also believed that it would protect the soul as well as the body, and would leave offerings at crossroads to placate their goddess of the Underworld, Hecate. When the garlic is cut or crushed, it allows the compound, alliin to combine with an enzyme, also found in garlic, allinase, to form the malodorous allicin. A similar process in its cousin allium, the onion, produces the tear-provoking reaction when cut. Allicin may smell bad, but this is just about the only antisocial thing about it.

The Egyptians are believed to have worshipped garlic, and clay model bulbs were found in Tutankhamun's tomb.

This compound, in turn, is transformed into diallyl sulphide, which is largely responsible for garlic's medicinal qualities: antibiotic, antifungal, bacteriostatic, bactericidal and a biological insecticide. Garlic also contains trace minerals; calcium, phosphorous and iron and is rich in vitamins B1 (thiamin) and vitamin C. Add to this the results from ongoing modern scientific research that show that garlic may deactivate carcinogens, suppressing the growth of tumours; that modern research has shown that it lowers blood cholesterol levels, preventing heart attacks, strokes and blood clots; that it promotes good circulation, and one could almost forgive its malodorous tendency.

One of the so-called 'Wet Trinity' of Indian cooking, *ginger*, takes its Latin generic name, Zingiber, from the Sanskrit for 'horn-shaped', *singabela*, emphasising this rhizome's similarity in appearance to deer antlers.

Ginger certainly warmed English hearts very quickly: almost every sauce recipe to survive from the Middle Ages lists it as an ingredient and Tudor England loved it, making it into sweetmeats, cakes and patties. It was said to have been a particular favourite of Henry VIII - perhaps because of its reputation at that time of being a powerful aphrodisiac! Gingerbread became popular in Elizabethan times and it became a popular practice in Victorian society to nibble crystallised ginger after a meal when it was disclosed that Chinese medicine recommended it for the digestion. British country folklore and 'white witchcraft' used it in a similar way to its not dissimilar cousin, galangal, in 'magic' spells, to enhance and strengthen their power and Culpeper, the astrologer-herbalist, assigned its ruler as the planet Mars, associated with fire and strength.

In South-East Asia, turmeric plays an important part in rituals and religious customs.

In Greek legend, Crocus was a beautiful young man who played a game of quoits with the messenger god, Mercury. One of the god's quoits hit Crocus on the head, killing him instantly. His friends grieved for him and where his blood had spilled on the grass, *saffron* crocuses sprang up. Probably because of the cost, giving it strong associations with wealth and power, saffron was attributed with ritual and caste significance, and was used to dye the robes of royalty and holy men and to produce the caste marks worn on the forehead in India, to where it was taken in around the 3rd century AD by the Moghuls. Herbalists have long been convinced of its powers as a digestive and appetite stimulant and in Persia, pregnant women traditionally wore a ball of saffron tied around the base of the stomach to ensure an easy delivery.

In South East Asia, *turmeric* plays an important part in rituals and religious customs: traditional weddings see it used as a dye for the arms of the bride and groom; Indonesians use turmeric water as a cologne; Malays believe that it offers protection from evil spirits and rub it on the stomachs of women who have given birth and on the umbilical cord of their infants. However, these practices are not just a question of superstition. Turmeric helps to calm inflammation and has an antibacterial action and, originally, its use in fish dishes was probably more for this latter property, preventing spoilage, than for any attractive colouring effect.

The spice mix lies at the heart of Indian cuisine, and understanding its constituents and the way each works with the other has occupied the thoughts and working hours of cooks and chefs throughout the world. They must also be cooked properly; raw spices can play havoc on the stomach lining.

Get it right and you have food fit for the gods; get it wrong and you not only have a taste disaster, but an uncomfortable time in the smallest room in the house!

The curry culture of Britain is full of wonderful stories and characters. The restaurant sector is not a cohesive entity and varies considerably according to religion, subcontinent origins and regional location in Britain, giving rise to the many variations that make the industry so exciting and fascinating.

'Authenticity' is a word much bandied about in the Asian food sector and one of the hardest to define as experience suggests there might be a mischievous twinkle in the eye when many Indian chefs and restaurateurs are holding forth on the subject.

We are told there is no such as thing a curry in India, until the British had introduced the word, they had never heard of it! Britain's favourite dish, Chicken Tikka Masala is not and never has been authentic - at least to India - just as Meat Madras is likewise totally unauthentic - at least to Madras. Vindaloo, Bindaloo or Tindaloo (who ever invented the latter two?) those ultimate arbiters of macho status are certainly not the dish that the Portuguese invented and Onion Bhaji - now, where did that come from?

The 'curry message' is promoted by celebrities and chefs from all over the world as well as the sub-continent

But then, who introduced all these words and dishes to an unsuspecting British public in the first place? Could it not be that the sector is market driven, just like most other successful industries? The truth is Indian cuisine is totally anarchic and is likely to stay so until an Indian Escoffier comes along, (Heaven forbid), and therein lays its excitement. Talk to most chefs or restaurateurs and you will find, with few exceptions, that *theirs* is the only authentic style and taste, and they do not have many polite words to say for their competitors. Others suggest that British Indian cuisine is an insult to Indian culture. However, it is a fact that almost all of the hard working people who have benefited with position and wealth beyond their wildest dreams actually come from the sub-continent - so who is insulting who?

The problem is that, for some reason, non-Asians in Britain have historically assumed that everyone hailing from India, Pakistan, Bangladesh or Sri Lanka, is an expert on all the foods of their home country. How many British or American people would like to make the same claim for their compatriots? Are you an expert

Simon Morris of Grafton Manor was the first non-Asian chef to win a major curry competition

on Haggis, Beef Wellington, Lancashire Hotpot, Parkin or Pheasant under Glass?

This attitude was very obvious in the early days of the introduction of Indian products into the supermarkets. Upon being asked how they chose the expert to act as consultant and creator of the new products, a very prominent supermarket chain told us, quite straight-faced, "why, the next lady through the door in a sari".

The huge range of knowledge needed to be an expert is such that very few can ever achieve that status. A very prominent restaurateur in Bradford who is happy to wax lyrical on the subject of authenticity even complained that the word 'chapatti' (a flat bread), although known and the bread consumed in Pakistan and India, certainly does not derive from either and

117

is another made-up name. In fact the chapatti is from Afghanistan - as are many words in Pakistan and North India, (understandably, as they share a border) - and refers to a bread made on a flat tawa rather than a tandoor. It can also be called 'nan-e-tawagi', although since that is a bit of a mouthful after a few lagers, we will happily stick to chapatti.

Sanjeev Kapoor, India's top TV chef is often asked whether his food is authentic, to which he replies, "It is authentic to Sanjeev Kapoor!"

In fact people from all over the sub-continent have used their own magic ingredients to weave their curry spell over the British consumer for many years now, and it is not surprising that such artistry has produced more than a few 'characters', and some tales of rivalry, some funny, others very much less so.

The huge range of knowledge you would need to become an expert (in Indian food) means that very few ever achieve that status.

The humorous side was acknowledged when a hilarious play by Sudha Bhuchar and Shaheen Khan, called Balti Kings, opened at the Lyric in Hammersmith in December 1999. The play is set in a kitchen in Birmingham's Baltiland where restaurants ruthlessly compete for business.

www.indiancookery.com

SANJEEV KAPOOR'S

KHANA KHAZANA

CELEBRATION OF INDIAN COOKERY

Sanjeev Kapoor - India's top TV chef

119

The action centres around Chef Billa, poached from Wembley, the owner's two sons, who have eyes on a Bollywood style re-opening, a lazy porter, sous-chef Yacoub and a little old lady who continually makes samosas and spouts the most horrific things directed against every sector of the community - including her own. When asked what a balti is, the restaurant owner responds, "Its a bucket, init? It's called balti because whities can't say karahi, init?". This sums up the response of many high street restaurants to the often very poor behaviour of many of their late night customers.

One restaurateur in Bath tried to stop a curry price slashing war only to be slashed himself -- literally.

On the more serious side you have the restaurant in London that objected to competition from its nearby neighbour, so set their kitchen alight; or the two restaurants side by side in Leicester that continually warned potential customers about the other restaurant, even to the extent of each posting libellous notices about the other in their windows; or the restaurateur in Bath who tried to stop a curry price slashing war only to be literally slashed himself by irate opponents on his own doorstep, only narrowly escaping death; or the drink company who sponsored a special event only to have all its promotional material torn down by a rival company; or even the trade magazine editor who had to go on the run to avoid a reported 'contract for a hit' after calling Indian waiters 'miserable gits' in print. There is no doubt about it, the industry is as varied, volatile and as exciting as the food it produces. From the fifties to the nineties, Indian waiters and restaurateurs expected little in terms of food knowledge from their customers. This is not to say that they treated their guests with contempt.

In fact, quite the reverse was true; in general, the restaurateur and his staff treated their customers with nothing but respect and received little politeness in return.

Over the years many Indian restaurants have sponsored local schools and football or cricket teams, and have raised thousands of pounds for local charities.

It is a testament to the character and resilience of the people in this hardworking and forbearing sector that they didn't throw up their hands in exasperation years ago and refuse to have anything further to do with the community at large. Instead of distancing themselves, however, they worked hard to ensure their acceptance by the local community. Including the name of the town in that of the restaurant was one of the early means of subtly becoming an integral part of the urban landscape, moving on to becoming involved with community works. Over the years many Indian restaurants

Indian restaurants raise thousands for charity. Kingfisher even organise World Curry Week for charity and Enam Ali's Le Raj is a regular contributor to this and other charities in common with hundreds of other restaurants.

121

have sponsored local schools and football or cricket teams, and have raised hundreds of thousands of pounds for local charities ranging from hospitals to community centres. When questioned on these activities, the restaurateur generally answers that community work is an integral part of their culture, especially the Muslims, whose almost universal answer seems to be that it is a duty in Islam.

That is not to say that the British love of curry does not have its detractors. Several Asian intellectuals, observing the very British style of Indian food served up and down the country, have accused the British of 'stealing their cultural and culinary heritage' but as Gary Rhodes and Gordon Ramsay are not accused of the same by the French, it would seem such an accusation has no real basis and is really part of the on-going debate that curry seems to generate. Also, the dishes, although formulated gradually for British tastes, are produced almost exclusively by Asians. One such critic even accused 'white' people of making huge profits on the back of 'their' culture. Hand on heart, we can state categorically that none of the 'white' people we know who work in and around the British curry scene (and there aren't many) are troubling the tax-man in any way whatsoever and, if they have Rolls Royces or Rolexes, they are keeping them pretty well hidden! So, why do we do it? The food and the industry are both addictive.

In the late eighties and nineties things began to change as the public became increasingly knowledgeable due to television programmes and spectator cookery. Again international travel also helped in this education process, with long-haul holidays package brochures beginning to offer Indian destinations. Supermarkets such as Tesco, Waitrose, Marks & Spencer, Asda and Sainsbury were stocking wider ranges of exotic herbs and spices, and an increasing selection of frozen and chilled products. It was not long before the ethnic chilled section became the quickest growing area in such supermarkets as the intrigued British public tried new dish after new dish. Curry fans were looking for more and now knew it existed.

Th food and the industry are both addictivee

The Wahhab Way

One-time national newspaper reporter, one-time editor of Tandoori Magazine, one-time public relations expert, the Iqbal Wahhab of old has metamorphosed into one of London's and Britain's top restaurateurs in a relatively short space of time.

With ancestral roots in Bangladesh, Iqbal is a self-taught food expert in common with many of our top chefs or restaurateurs in other sectors.

In his time at Tandoori he was a great supporter of the industry but never afraid to shine a light in whatever he considered to be a dark corner, and it was one such well-meaning but possibly poorly expressed revelation that caused him to abandon his journalistic profession and go under cover. That is several years ago but the industry still seems to be split between fans and extreme enemies. Iqbal Wahhab, however, is made of sterner stuff and he was soon back with, first, Tabla in Docklands, and then his Cinnamon Club concept in the old Westminster Library near the Houses of Parliament with future plans for a British restaurant, a bar and expansion in America.

Cinnamon Club was born amidst a feeding frenzy of media coverage, some of it casting doubt on the concept but all of it revolving around Iqbal himself. Stand or fall it was his dream, his baby.

Chef Vivek Singh was the most important cog in his wheel and it was the very excitement that Iqbal generated around the project that made Vivek decide to accept the London post.

One of the biggest assets of Cinnamon Club, now one of the top Indian restaurants in the country is its multi-national staff. Without exception, they buy into Iqbal's vision of a cuisine that grows and develops continually. Such is their affection for their outspoken boss that they have even created a cocktail in his name - The Wahhab

Way - Absolut Vodka, citron and sugar - a definite pick-me-up. Iqbal Wahhab does not possess the innate, set in stone beliefs of some other restaurateurs and chefs. His is a fluid philosophy and he has complete belief in what he says at the time he says it. In his time as a journalist he argued against red-flocked wallpaper, bad wine lists, poor service, miserable waiters and lack of menu variation. Indeed if you sat down and talked to him now, he would be more than happy to point out the shortcomings of the industry as seen from his own unique viewpoint. In Cinnamon Club he had the rare opportunity of changing thought to deed by demonstrating first hand exactly what he meant. It is his continual flow of new ideas

and concepts and his distinctive laugh and personality that have drawn the great and good to him and he remains a consummate public relations manipulator of the first order.

The up-market end of the industry grew apace and the movers and shakers became very evident, each providing an invaluable lead to a sector that works hard, long hours and cannot individually spare time to research new market trends.

The move up-market of the Indian restaurant sector has often been attributed to establishment of *The Bombay Brasserie*, not far from Gloucester Road Tube Station in London. The restaurant was the concept of Camellia Panjabi, (sister of Namita Panjabi of Chutney Mary fame), then of Taj International Hotels and she pressed ahead with the project in spite of being warned that it was doomed to failure. It was opened between Hotels Gloucester and Baileys, opposite Gloucester Road tube station on 10th December 1982; an auspicious date decided on by top astrologer Mr Sohoni who fixed it date after much deliberation, with Sagittarius in the ascendant at dawn and Gemini at dusk. The gloom merchants could not have been more wrong and, run by Adi Modi with Manager Arun Harnal and Head Chef Udit Sarkhel (to be replaced by Vikram Sunderam when he left to start his own venture), the BB has gone on to set the standard many other Indian restaurants strive for. The restaurant serves 260 diners in colonial splendour and has been visited by politicians, film stars and celebrities from all walks of life. The atmosphere is very special, the service top class with food to match.

The move up-market of the Indian restaurant sector has often been attributed to establishment of The Bombay Brasserie

Reflecting the change in the Indian restaurant sector, a sister restaurant, *Quilon*, was opened by Adi Modi in 1999 alongside the Crowne Plaza St James Court Hotel as the second Taj restaurant venture in the UK, the first

for seventeen years. Managed by the extremely professional Richard Hand, (unfortunately now deceased), the smart new restaurant was totally unlike its sister Bombay Brasserie; it introduced superb South Indian food of a high standard, prepared by Head Chef A.V. Sriram another ex-Taj Hotels chef with a unique touch, underlining the industry's move to regional cuisine. The food is light and extremely well spiced to create layers of taste. The wine list is particularly well organised and presented and the whole experience is special, from the rasam to the Mangalorean Chicken.

Chutney Mary became the first up-market Indian restaurant to promote Anglo-Indian cuisine.

Chutney Mary, the brainchild of Cambridge educated and one-time merchant banker Namita Panjabi, opened in 1990 to become the first up-market Indian restaurant to promote Anglo-Indian cuisine. Namita had had a life-long passion for real Indian food, and travelled throughout the length and breadth of India to find it. Her belief is that the best Indian food is not found in conventional restaurants in India, but in peoples' homes, maharajas' palaces, and humble wayside stalls. Namita and husband Ranjit Mathrani created Chutney Mary, located in Chelsea, London, which won the Award of the Best Indian Restaurant in the UK shortly afterwards. Initially they based the menu on Anglo-Indian gems such as Bangalore Bangers and Mash, (Chutney Mary was a name for an Anglo-Indian woman in the days of the Raj). Time and experience, however, convinced Namita that the British public were ready to explore other aspects of Indian cuisine and they have moved the menu on, leaving behind the colonial, and introducing regional dishes never seen before on British restaurant menus.

The very popular Chutney Mary in Chelsea

They again transformed Chutney Mary in May 2002 to ensure it remained one of Britain's finest restaurants serving Indian food. They bought *Veeraswamy*, UK's oldest surviving Indian restaurant situated close to Piccadilly Circus, London, in 1997 when rumours abounded that it might have to close down. They totally refashioned it, which then won it the award of the Best Indian Restaurant by Time Out, the leading London lifestyle magazine. In 2001 they saw another niche market and opened *Masala Zone*, a fun, innovative and casual Indian restaurant located in Soho, London W1. It has proved so popular that they have opened a second Masala Zone in Islington, London N1. At the opposite end of the price scale to their older sisters, these two newer restaurants serve real Indian food at unreal prices - under £13 per head - in a sleek tribal art setting.

It was once said that Cyrus Todiwala (see feature on pages 140-141) is to Indian cuisine in Britain what Gordon Ramsay is to French. If that means that they are both naturally gifted chefs at the top of their particular sector and have a problem suffering fools gladly, then perhaps the comparison is reasonable. Todiwala of *Café Spice Namaste* was certainly the first of the Indian 'celebrity' chefs and remains one of the great and most knowledgeable characters in the industry.

Iqbal Wahhab (see feature on pages 124-125) is not and never has been a chef but must be one of the best known people in the Indian Restaurant sector and a figure that seems to bring forth comment from most people you might ask, (and even sometimes from people you don't ask), some of it quietly supportive, a lot of it, unfortunately negative (or perhaps jealous!). Moving somewhat forcibly from trade magazine editor to restaurateur, his long delayed *Cinnamon Club* project opened amidst a blaze of publicity, including a TV documentary, and wild claims that he was going to show restaurants how to produce proper Indian food. Iqbal no longer makes wild claims for his concept, having modified his ideas a little to make them more accessible to his customers but with a £5 million annual turnover, he has proved his point and remains at the cutting edge of the industry.

Zaika was to be Claudio Pulze's first Indian restaurant venture and it was well known he expected all his restaurants to be Michelin recognised.

Top : Cyrus & Pervin Todiwala of Café Spice Namaste
Left : Vineet Bhatia once of Zaika now of Rasoi Vineet Bhatia
Right : Atul Kochhar of Benares

The Indian restaurant sector had really come of age when two London establishments achieved a coveted Michelin star in the same year. Oberoi trained Chef Vineet Bhatia was enticed away from fashionable Star of India by entrepreneur Claudio Pulze. *Zaika* was to be Claudio's first Indian restaurant venture and it was well known that he expected all his restaurants, regardless of the style of cuisine, to be Michelin recognised. Vineet was soon creating his own very individual style which was frowned upon by many Indian cuisine purists but which excited the culinary fraternity at large. One wag even went as far as dubbing the style, 'Mediterr-Indian', in a sideswipe reference to Claudio's influence on Vineet's food. At the same time Chef Atul Kochhar, also Oberoi trained, was developing his own style at *Tamarind* in Mayfair whilst Rajesh Suri created a front of house worthy of any top class restaurant in the world. Atul left Tamarind to open his own restaurant -Benares- in August 2002 but such were the standards at Tamarind that it retained its Michelin star status with new Head Chef Alfred Prasad. Bhatia also left the restaurant where he won his Michelin star just over a year later to open his own Rasoi Vineet Bhatia.

Tamarind Head Chef Alfred Prasad

The huge influence both Tamarind and Zaika had on an industry that, historically, had been used to a small dark corner in the culinary hall of fame, was that it illustrated the diversity of Indian cuisine and the recognition that could be achieved at the highest level.

132

One of the few examples of a successful restaurant concept starting in India then being recreated in London is *Chor Bizarre* (Thieves Market!), opened in 1997 by Mahendra Kaul of Gaylord fame in partnership with Rohit Khattar, who owns the restaurant of a similar name in New Delhi. The 80-seater restaurant is a treasure trove of traditional Indian delights, all of which you may buy - but you might a have trouble carrying the bed-table out of the door! Each table is different - and exquisite - as are the chairs, some of which take the form of arch-necked horses and stocky elephants. Understandably, the decor fascinates diners almost as

Rohit Khattar at the opening of Chai Bizarre the specialist tea and tiffin section of London's Chor Bizarre.

much as the very individual style of food provided by the kitchen team. Frequented by many discerning personalities such as Ismail Merchant, the Indian Film Producer and Director, dining here is a unique experience. London has tended to be the cauldron for changes in most cuisines in Britain (except for balti!) given its cosmopolitan market, and it is not surprising that many of the top names in the industry are based there. People like Amin Ali of *Red Fort,* Mehernosh and Sherin Mody of the fabulous *La Porte des Inde s*, both ex-Taj and both international chefs in their own right, (although Sherin concentrates on front of house for La

133

Porte and the equally fabulous *Thai Blue Elephant* Restaurant these days), Andy Varma of *Vama* onetime haunt of Sir Richard Branson whose wife Joan said to him, "you might as well move your bed there", and other 'luvvies', Das Sreedharan whose four *Rasa* restaurants bring the wonders of South Indian food to London, Navin Bhatia of the *Cafe Lazeez Group* (the restaurant chain credited with starting new wave Indian), the popular *Bombay Palace* in Connaught Street and many others, have all had their influence - but one has stood the test of time more than most.

In 1955 when *Star of India* on Brompton Road opened, it offered meat curry or fish curry with chips, rice or even half chips/half rice. In 1995, celebrating its ruby anniversary, the excellence and top class nature of the food at Star of India, was as telling an indication of how restaurants had evolved and improved over recent decades as you could possibly find.

In 1955 when Star of India in Brompton Road opened it offered Meat Curry or Fish Curry with chips.

Much of the credit for the restaurant's pre-eminence goes to owner/manager Reza Mahammad, who is passionate about his family's business. Reza, one of the industry's most amazing, colourful and flamboyant characters (you ought to see him in full Indian regalia), is responsible for the Italian style frescoes which decorate the walls and ceilings, and for encouraging the chefs such as Vineet Bhatia, who worked here after arriving from Oberoi Hotels in India en route to his Michelin star, to break new ground and provide the customers with something new and exciting. The exterior of the restaurant is not terribly imposing but once inside you are in Reza's world. Everything is slightly over the top but in such a way that has aficionados flocking to its doors night after night.

Top left: Bombay Palace W2
Above: Navin Bhatia of Café Lazeez
Left: Kuldeep Singh of Mela Shaftesbury
Avenue and Chowki
Below: Mehernosh and Shireen Alexander
Mody's La Porte des Indes near Marble Arch

Kuldeep Singh's London background does not go back quite that far but he has certainly made his unique mark on the Indian restaurant scene in Britain. He initially came to London from Taj Hotels to work in Amin Ali's Red Fort in Soho. His next venture took him to Trevor Gulliver's new Pukkabar in Sydenham (sadly no longer with us) as an attempt, although short-lived, to create the 'curry pub'. His big success came when he opened *Mela* in Shaftesbury Avenue creating a new style that Evening Standard critic Fay Maschler was totally in support of. His efforts to change the Indian restaurant scene continued when *Chowki* was opened near Piccadilly within the 'Mela Group', also with Fay's blessing and support, and his latest opening takes the location to Manchester.

One of the undisputed top Indian chefs in Britain plies his trade in Southfields, SW18, not far from the world famous Wimbledon Lawn Tennis Club. Udit Ranjan Sarkhel was born in Jamshadpur, India on 31st July 1958. After a three years degree from Calcutta University and a Diploma in Hotel Management and Catering Technology in Bombay he joined the Taj Group of Hotels in 1981 as Trainee Chef. By 1984 he was Head Chef in the specialist Tanjore Restaurant and had travelled extensively all over India. He also organised food promotions in such far flung places as Hong Kong, Singapore and Paris for his employers so it was no great surprise when, in May 1988 he was appointed Executive Chef at the, by now, hugely popular Bombay Brasserie in London where his cooking attracted the great and the good. In 1997 he and his hotel and catering management-trained wife Veronica, decided to go it alone and opened *Sarkhel's* in Replingham Road. People knew it was to be something special from the start because Udit is that rare entity, a true artist. He does not stand aloof but likes to interact with his customers. "Ten years ago," he says, "many people would not have known the reasons behind what they are eating - not so today". He is a chef who can't stay out of the kitchen, and long may that continue.

136

Above : Andy Varma's Vama - The Indian Room in Chelsea
Below : Udit Sarkhel's restaurant - Sarkhel's in Southfields

*Left to right :Arun Harnal, Chef Vikram Sunderam and Adi Modi of Bombay Brasserie and below
the wonderful lunchtime buffet in the restaurant's conservatory*

Moving outside London to Epsom Downs, Surrey you find *Le Raj*, opened in 1991. Le Raj has always been known for being something different in Indian cuisine and a culinary beacon for the Bangladeshi sector. Owned by Guild of Bangladeshi Restaurateurs founder Enam Ali, an ex-International Indian Chef of the Year, it offers a very individual style of food and drink in very stylish surroundings and has 'foodies' coming from far and wide to check it out. Celebrities abound from 007 star Pierce Brosnan to TV celebrity and ex DJ Chris Tarrant, who hosts a special 'Help a Capital London Child' function there every year. Enam's lead has caused many other Bangladeshi restaurants to start the move up-market, away from the red-flocked wallpaper and one-pot masala menus of days gone by.

Further afield in Buckinghamshire you will find one of the greatest examples of how the industry is changing. "The new *Jaipur* is not mine," said owner Abdul Ahad as he opened his great new project, "it belongs to the people of Milton Keynes." A cunning piece of marketing, you might say, but the words reflect a feeling he and his colleagues honestly hold that this landmark restaurant, the largest purpose-built Indian establishment in Europe, identifies with the city and community.

Ahad started off his career in the area in 1980 at the Milton Keynes Tandoori in Bletchley. He went on to win almost every award offered by numerous curry guides at his original Jaipur, near the railway station in Milton Keynes. Built in two stories with a domed feature, many thought the new building was to be a Mosque instead of one of the most ambitious restaurant projects you are ever likely to find looking like some fabled Indian palace.

Bradford has a long association with the curry industry and a proud, largely Pakistani and Kashmiri restaurant industry, supported by a strong Asian community.

Above : Enam Ali (third from left) hosts Chris Tarrant and 'Help a London Child' at Le Raj in Epsom

Below : Abdul Ahad's fabulous Jaipur in Milton Keynes

Cyrus Todiwala MBE

Cyrus Rustom Todiwala was born and brought up in Bombay, now Mumbai, and graduated from Bombay's Catering College to train as a

chef with the famous Taj Group in India. As with all Taj chefs, his grounding was across the spectrum but his particular forte was as a patissière. His training continued from 1976 to 1980 when he went to the Geneva Intercontinental as a sous chef for a short time, before becoming chef de partie at Chambers Club until 1982.

This was followed by two years as chef de cuisine at Taj Holiday Village and from 1984 to 1989 he was Executive Chef at Fort Aguada Beach Resort, The Aguada Hermitage and The Taj Holiday Village, catering for Heads of State and even royalty. It was during this time he was appointed Wild Life Warden for Goa by the Chief Minister and Lieutenant Governor, and became a founder member for conservation of endangered species.

In 1989 he went into his first restaurant venture as a working partner in The Place, whilst designing and equipping kitchens and learning about Thai and Singapore cuisine.

In 1991 Cyrus and his wife Pervin, also formally trained in the culinary skills, moved to London. Cyrus became Executive Chef at Namaste Restaurant in Alie Street E1.

In 1993 he took over as Chef/Director of Namaste with the help of Pervin, and continued to offer dishes not seen in Indian restaurants elsewhere in Britain to considerable critical acclaim. It was during this period he met entrepreneur Michael Gottlieb of Smollensky's fame and the two hit it off immediately. In 1995 the smart Café Spice Namaste opened in nearby Prescot Street, in an old listed building offering acres of room.

Cyrus is the complete chef and has even helped start and operate The Asian and Oriental School of Catering to which he gives considerable time in an effort to pass on his knowledge. He talks animatedly about his aims and dreams and pauses to answer a shrilling phone. Someone needs 10 tonnes of a herb they cannot source. Hang on says Cyrus, calls Bombay, and the order is sealed within seconds, with hardly a break in what we were discussing prior to the call. After a hectic day at Café Spice he was off to the Parsee, their other restaurant in Highgate, whose menu and basic food is prepared by Cyrus' team.

His success is based on his natural ability and his background. He is like a test pilot. He will bubble over with excitement at the creation of a new dish, which may or may not work, or the sourcing of a new product. He will try anything from bison to crocodile - "that didn't really work," he says, with a disarming grin.

He has appeared on numerous radio and television programmes and since 1999 has also been a member of the National Advisory Council for Education and Training Targets.

In August 2000 he received a very deserved MBE in recognition of his services to the catering industry.

Mumtaz Restaurant, a division of Mumtaz Food Industries Ltd, was established in Bradford, West Yorkshire in 1980 and has built an excellent reputation and a huge following over the years. As with several restaurants in Bradford, it observes a strictly no alcohol policy and originally catered for 150 diners offering the Mumtaz style of 'authentic' Kashmiri/Indian cuisine. As with many major Indian restaurants, it went on to develop a manufacturing side, producing top class products for the specialist Indian food market. During the last year or so Mumtaz Restaurant has undergone major redevelopment and expansion, which greatly increased its seating capacity and made it one of the smartest Asian restaurants in Europe. The largest at the time of writing is

Aakash in Cleckheaton at over 800 although there are claims from *Anam's* in Bradford and the *Nawaab* in Levenshulme of over 1000! Until these came along *Crème de la Crème* in Glasgow had been secure in its title with 600 seats for several years. The outskirts of Bradford are also home to the hugely successful *Aagrah Group* of restaurants. The first Aagrah restaurant was opened in July 1977 in the small Airedale town of Shipley, offering Asian cuisine in the Kashmiri style. Such was the reception of the Aagrah that it soon became nationally and internationally recognised.

The Aakash in Cleckheaton

The special qualities found in the Shipley restaurant were then developed further afield in Pudsey (1986), Skipton (1989), Garforth (1993), Doncaster (1995), Tadcaster (1996) and Wakefield (1997) followed by Denby Dale and the glittering Leeds branch in 2004. The Aagrah restaurants are

Mohammed Aslam (right) & his brother Mohammed Sabir of the Aagrah Group

Aagrah Shipley

personally managed by the Sabir family, whose desire is to offer 'authentic' dishes as prepared in their homeland, coupled with the highest standard of friendly service.

143

Mohammed Aslam, the youngest brother of the family and once a smiling bus driver, won the International Indian Chef of the Year award in 1995 and has continued to mastermind the group ever since, including the ambitious development of their new headquarters at Shipley, which now fronts a completely new manufacturing plant for retail products. Aagrah's success has certainly pointed the way for others to follow in the north of England.

Mohammed Aslam, the youngest brother of the family and once a bus driver, won the International Indian Chef of the Year title in 1995 and now runs the Aagrah Group.

Dr Wali Tasar Uddin MBE

The curry industry is also alive and well in Scotland and some of the industry's greatest fans hail from there. In Edinburgh, restaurateur and cookery book author Tommy Miah, created The *International Chef of the Year Competition* that has grown in prominence over its more than ten years of existence. Meanwhile, fellow Leith restaurateur, Dr Wali Tasar Uddin MBE has opened several restaurants in the city, culminating in the fabulous award-winning *Britannia Spice*, named after the famous royal yacht, now a tourist

attraction, moored just yards away. As the Honorary Consul for
Bangladesh in Scotland, he is also the sector's elder statesman in the
region, also steering the British Bangladesh Chamber of Commerce to
greater heights as its Director-General.

The saucy and stylish Kama Sutra restaurant tempted diners to 'indulge in the food of love.....from every angle.'

In Glasgow the Harlequin Restaurant Group Empire started in 1984, when
Charan Gill MBE and his business
partner, Master Chef Gurmail
Dhillon purchased the '*Ashoka West
End*' in the Kelvingrove area of
Glasgow.
Soon we saw the arrival of the '*Spice
of Life*' and hot on its trail, two
Ashokas, in Ashton Lane, the South
Side of the city, and Johnstone. By
1996 the saucy and stylish '*Kama
Sutra*' restaurant opened in
November in the heart of the city
centre, tempting diners to 'indulge
in the food of love'...from every
angle. September 1997 saw the
arrival of the great *Ashoka* name in
Bearsden and Kirkintilloch, and in
December 1997, Bellshill,
Lanarkshire, saw the opening of

Charan Gill MBE

145

'The Shieling Complex' - the complete Indo-Scottish experience! Upstairs, is the sassy 'Ashoka Bellshill'; downstairs, in dramatic contrast, is the 'Whisky Galore' Bar Diner - inspired by Charan's coveted collection of whisky bottles salvaged from the wreck of the S.S. Politician, which sank off Eriskay in 1941. By May, 1998 '*Mister Singh's* India' in Charing Cross became part of the Group and, within months, it was converted from a traditional style restaurant to a stunning example of contemporary chic. In February 2000, the '*Ashoka at the Mill*' opened amidst a blaze of publicity situated in a 250-seater medieval millhouse. A new and adventurous addition to the Group, the '*Ashoka Shak'* opened in March 2001 in the Phoenix Leisure Park in Linwood, Renfrewshire and signified a new genre for the Harlequin Group.

If you are looking for curry characters, Glasgow is full of them. Look no further than Raj Bhajwe, General Manager of the hugely successful Café India in Charing Cross - and the only Indian restaurateur we know of with

Raj welcomes Tom Jones

an Equity card. Celebrities galore have visited the popular restaurant at Raj's behest and he gets regular visits from superstar Michael Jackson whenever he is in town. Such is their relationship that, if Michael cannot get to Glasgow on a particular visit, Raj will fly down to London for a chat! The list of stars who have patronised the restaurant is endless, for which Raj will provide photographic evidence, given a little nudging.

Raj Bhajwe, general manager of the hugely successful Café India is the only Indian restaurateur we know of with an Equity card.

Like many aspects of British society, the Indian restaurant industry is a place of hard work, intrigue, laughter, disappointment and the occasional excess. Throughout the nation 'curry streets' have grown up, each with their own individual character and restaurants opening next door to each other as members of the same family grouping try to cash in on the success of their established relations.

Brick Lane, London

Brick Lane is the centre of the curry restaurant industry in East London and one of the most famous curry areas in Britain. The area is historically famous for providing refuge to those fleeing persecution. In the 18th century the area was occupied by silk weavers, largely descended from the Huguenot refugees, (French Protestants escaping from Catholic persecution in France). A hundred years later, Jews fleeing the pogroms in Eastern Europe, founded a thriving community, adding their tailoring skills to the industrial make-up of the area. But nowhere is the unique history of the area better depicted than in the history of the local mosque.

London's famous Brick Lane

The mosque in Brick Lane has been a place of worship for different faiths for hundreds of years. Initially built as church by the Huguenots, it was converted to a synagogue when a largely Jewish community replaced the protestant population. By the middle of the 20th century the Jewish community had mostly moved on and the building was converted again, this time into a mosque to serve the Bangladeshi community. With its culture and cuisine the Bangladeshi influence gives a cosmopolitan feel to Spitalfields. The influence is so striking that the area has been dubbed Bangla Town.

Brick Lane is one of the few curry streets where waiters actually stand outside and tout for business on occasions (although this has caused problems recently) and it is on many a tourist 'must see' list when visiting London. A sizeable percentage of the more than 160,000 Bangladeshis currently in Britain live in and around the East End, pushing out into the Home Counties. You can find it all in Brick Lane. Exotic supermarkets such as the Taj, modern, sleek restaurants such as *Cafe Naz* and *The Clifton* and a wealth of others, some of which still live in a nostalgic curry time warp.

Belgrave Road/London Road, Leicester

Leicester has the distinction of having two curry streets, both very different in nature. The Belgrave Road area of Leicester was a barren wasteland when the Ugandan Asians arrived and were resettled there. They took this run-down section of the city and created a vibrant, colourful street stretching out into the suburbs; the now famous curry road that houses sari shops, jewellers and fabulous restaurants

149

and is home to Jains and Hindus in the main. You can try wonderful vegetarian food at *Bobby's* or *Thali*, Kenyan Punjabi food at *Curry Fever* or a wider variety of fayre at *Curry Pot* or *Friends*. On the other side of town, London Road is the home to most of the Bangladeshi and other Indian, restaurants catering more for the carnivore than the vegetarian, such as *Shimla Pinks* and *The Tiffin*. The combination gives the curry fan the chance of experiencing the foods of several different regions of the sub-continent in one city.

The Balti Triangle, Birmingham

Off to Birmingham, and their curry street is actually *three* streets, forming the Balti Triangle. Ladypool Road, Stoney Lane and Stratford Road are littered with bright, brash, mainly balti restaurants that really buzz when night falls. Brummies take the balti factor very seriously indeed, and the Association of Balti Restaurateurs have long lobbied for a dedicated college to teach new generations the 'mysteries' of the Birmingham balti. Indian restaurants are prevalent throughout the city in places such as Broad Street and Hagley Road and standards range from the swish *Shimla Pinks*, *Rajdoot*, *Coconut Lagoon*, *Barajee* or *Cafe Lazeez* in the new Mailbox Complex, to the most basic 'Joe's caff' balti restaurant. The media have been fascinated

Café Lazeez, Birmingham

150

with the balti boom but signs are that Birmingham has not turned its back on other, more up-market Indian styles whilst maintaining its grip on its very own, fun-style balti cuisine.

Wilmslow Road, Manchester

Manchester is home to Pakistani and Kashmiri food, much like Bradford, which does not really have its own 'curry street', with restaurants scattered around like a fallout from a bomb blast. Not so Manchester where Wilmslow Road in the Rusholme district, the Curry Mile, is probably the most famous of the 'curry streets' sitting easily alongside Brick Lane in the hallowed halls of curry fame. In this Asian cultural quarter of Manchester the curry buff can choose from nearly fifty restaurants and takeaways, catering for all taste preferences and pockets and the restaurants are hugely popular. Since the first restaurants appeared in the late 1960's the area has steadily grown to become regarded as one of the most fun and exciting areas for Asian cuisine in the country. Rusholme is also known for its jewellery, fashion and other specialist retailers. This one-mile stretch of business offers a one-stop opportunity to shop and eat in unique culturally rich surroundings. Part of the attraction of Rusholme involves taking in this unique atmosphere by peering into windows piled high with sticky sweets - check out the Sanam Sweet House - and perusing the multitudinous array of menus with their individual nuances, influences and styles. The choice includes TV documentary stars like

Royal Naz, Rusholme, Manchester

151

The Darbar and the plush *Shere Khan*, who also own an outlet in the Trafford Centre and others outside the city. Nighat Awan OBE's Shere Khan group now also sells curry sauces in branded jars in supermarket chains nationwide and abroad.

Other good examples include *The Dil Dar* and the *Lal Halweli,* which combines delicious food with entertainment, employing a resident magician every night except Sunday and Monday. You'll pay higher prices - but never excessively so - at places such as the modern and chic *Hanaan* or the *Sangam.* The bill will be much lower at the ever-popular *Shezan* - not to be confused with its equally excellent but more expensive sister across the road. There's even a specialist ice-cream outlet, *Moonlight,* serving specialist desserts and drinks like Faluda, a sweet, creamy concoction with sweet vermicelli noodles and Lassi, yoghurt-based spicy or sweet drinks.

During the day the excitement is muted but at night, the street is a riot of neon, with hoards of curry fans pouring into restaurants such as *Shere Khan,* up-market, one time favourite of Coronation Street stars, and *Royal Naz,* a colourful restaurant, boasting an open kitchen that never seems to be closed. Situated opposite the Darbar, Royal Naz colourful boss Foysol and his chef wife Azera Parveen have often had less than cordial relationships with their opposite number over Chef of the Year claims in this publicity-seeking sector of Manchester. One thing they all have in common, however, is tremendous value for money that makes Rusholme a Mecca for curry fans.

Oxford, Southall, Wembley, Glasgow

Other cities have smaller versions of 'curry streets' that help travelling curry fans zero in on to experience a new restaurant. Oxford has Cowley Road; Southall, London's great centre of Punjabi food in general and Kenyan Punjabi in particular, The Broadway ; Wembley, High Road, Ealing

Road and Harrow Road; Nottingham, Mansfield Road and Alfreton Road; Cardiff, Cowbridge Road East and Albany Road; Glasgow, Sauchiehall Street and Argyle Street in King's' Cross, (where curry is so popular that Café India achieved a massive record total of nearly 1200 customers in one twelve hour period). Each 'curry street' has its own unique character and offers the curry fan a wide variety of cultural and culinary experiences.

Top : Aziz, Oxford
Below : Brilliant, Southall
Right : Café India, Glasgow

154 **Chapter 5** Curry on Eating

Queens, politicians, celebrities - curry has endeared itself to every level of British society and there are thousands of curry clubs championing its cause. Critics, awards, charity and social events, books and magazines all combine to ensure the growth of curry culture continues.

"Curry and Rice on Forty Plates:
Or the Ingredients of Social Life at Our Station in India"
Author: Captain George F. Atkinson
First published by Day & Son, London in 1854

What varied opinions we constantly hear

Of our rich oriental possessions

What a jumble of notions, distorted and queer

From an Englishman's Indian impressions.

First a sun, fierce and glaring, that scorches and bakes

Plankeens, perspiration and worry

Mosquito tugs, coconut, Brahmins and snakes

With elephants, tigers and curry.

Curry has become a part of the fabric of everyday life in Britain, and has fascinated the British as no other cuisine or pastime has ever done in history. It has been suggested that more people are curry fans than follow any one religion or sport in this country of some 60 million souls, and it does appear to be true that most people can name their favourite curry dish or favourite Indian restaurant.

The media have also become fascinated with the phenomenon, glorifying in the industry's occasional little scandals, and many a miracle cure has been claimed for its ingredients: Curry *'may slow Alzheimer's'*; *'Curry is a cancer fighter'*; Curry *'may treat radiation burns'*; *'Curry is an aphrodisiac'*. Quite apart from these claims, which seem to appear at regular intervals - usually on slow news days - it would seem that curry has its supporters in every walk of life and at every level of society.

Curry Celebrities

*"Playwrights are like men who have been dining for a month in an Indian restaurant.
After eating curry night after night, they deny the existence of asparagus."*
Peter Ustinov, Christian Science Monitor

*"This curry was like a performance of Beethoven's Ninth Symphony that I'd once
heard... especially the last movement, with everything screaming and banging 'Joy.' It
stunned, it made one fear great art. My father could say nothing after the meal."*
Anthony Burgess

Curry is a familiar scent in the halls of power in Britain. Her Majesty, The
Queen, has been reported to have ordered a discreet takeaway to share
with the corgies, and we have already documented the enthusiasm of
Queen Victoria for the odd Indian meal! The Queen Mother was said to
have liked to partake on occasion - even after her centenary. Prime
Minister Tony Blair and wife Cherie are regularly in the news with their
Indian takeaway activities. They even arranged for an Indian catering
company to provide Indian food at one of their Number 10 staff garden
parties.

In case you think this is rare
for a Prime Minister, John
and Norma Major were not
averse to the odd visit to
their local curry house in
Huntingdon, and Baroness
Thatcher certainly enjoyed
sending her chauffeur out
for her favourite Indian
food.

*Laurence Dallaglio puts in an appearance at London's Bengal
Clipper*

157

Café India's Raj Bhajwe with celebrity Matt Goss

The Houses of Parliament are even said to have their own curry club, with almost half the MP's listed as members, and it's true that you can almost certainly see more of the nation's representatives in restaurants such as *Red Fort, Kundan* or *Cinnamon Club* than in the House of Commons on occasion.

MP enthusiasts include Keith Vaz and Frank Dobson, both regular Red Fort visitors, Michael Portillo, Kenneth Clark, Edwina Currie (of course), Paddy Ashdown, David Steel, Emma Nicholson, Neil Kinnock, London's Mayor Ken Livingstone and many others.

The Bombay Brasserie alone lists a glittering array of stars, including Vanessa Redgrave, Maggie Smith, Jeanne Moreau, Felicity Kendal, Tom Stoppard, Emma Thompson, Helena Bonham-Carter, Hugh Grant, Charlton Heston, Bruce Springsteen, Telly Savalas, all three screen Godfathers, Al Pacino, Robert De Niro and Marlon Brando, Tom Hanks, Kurt Russell, Goldie Hawn, Michael Caine, Sir Anthony Hopkins of Hannibal Lector fame,

158

Chef to the stars Andy Varma of Vama The Indian Room in Chelsea poses with Jamiroqwuoi (top left), Nicky from Westlife (top right), model Jodie Kidd (bottom left) and Martine McCutcheon (bottom right)

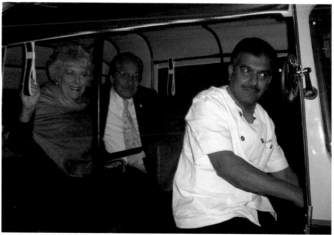

Chef Udit Sarkhel of Sarkhel's in Southfields gives actor, cook and celebrity Saeed Jaffrey and wife Jennifer a lift in a put put at a fundraiser

159

Tom Cruise and Nicole
Kidman, together and apart
- need we go on!
Beatles George Harrison
and Paul McCartney were
curry fans as are Elton John,
George Michael, Shirley

John Inverdale talks to Nassar Hussain & Sebastian Coe at a Bengal Clipper fundraiser

Bassey, Three Degrees, Tom
Jones, Cliff Richard, Donny
Osmond and even Michael Jackson.
Sport and curry have long gone hand in hand and hardly a cricketer or
footballer is immune, with whole teams falling under its spell. Snooker has
its share, with stars Jimmy White, Steve Davis, David Taylor and Willy
Thorne all partial to the odd curry. Football too gets in on the act, with
Terry Venables, Ally McCoist, Gary Lineker and Lee Dixon, who even had
shares in an Indian restaurant amongst his business interests.

Discussions about curry, its ingredients, cooking methods and, of course, favourite restaurants, seem to generate almost as much heat as the curries themselves

Stories of celebrity curry diners abound, ranging from Ian Botham, Nick
Faldo and even Keith Floyd to Rowan Atkinson, Andrew Lloyd-Webber,
Brooke Shields, Jane Seymour, Sharon Stone, 007 Pierce Brosnan and
superstar Mel Gibson.

160

Café India, Glasgow - home to the stars.

Top left : Film star Keanu Reeves
Top right : Footballer & TV personality Ally McCoist
Middle : Raj Bhajwe(left) and owner Dr. Abdul Sattar welcome Sir Cliff Richard
Bottom left : Pop group Maroon Five

161

Entrepreneur Sir Richard Branson was, at one time, so keen on Andy Varma of Vama's in Chelsea that when he wasn't passing a pleasant hour or two at the restaurant, he turned the tables by having Andy at his house to cook for the odd private dinner party. Restaurateur and cookery book writer Tommy Miah was even clever enough to take advantage of the celebrity love of curry when producing a cookery book for Cancer Research UK. Contributors included *Alan Ball (Lamb Rogan Josh), Cherie Blair (Kutchi Bhindi), Chicken Tikka (Sir Richard Branson), Sir Tom Farmer, founder of Kwikfit, (Fish Dopiaza), Glenda Jackson (Saag Aloo), Tom Jones (Prawn Curry), Kevin Keegan (Chicken Tikka Masala), Victoria Wood (Vegetable Curry), and Neil Kinnock (Vegetable Bhaji).*

Tommy Miah at the opening of his restaurant in Bangladesh

Curry Clubs

The British have a habit of uniting together in groups with a common cause, and curry would seem to be just one such cause. There are thousands of curry clubs all over Britain. From churches to football clubs, businesses to pub groups such as J.D. Weatherspoon, curry clubs abound and everyone seems to be an expert! Discussions about curry, dish ingredients and cooking methods and, of course, favourite restaurants, seem to generate almost as much heat as the curries themselves.

The Curry Club, the original body to have borne the name, was inaugurated in 1962 by a like-minded group, many of whom were employed on the Barbican project. The Curry Club is a Gentleman's dining club, managed by a committee that is elected from the membership. Meetings are held on the last Friday of alternate months, commencing in January. They meet at the *India Club*, Strand Continental Hotel, London and meetings are formal, with addresses by the president and others, and a loyal toast. They have a strict dress code; all are expected to wear a jacket and tie, and members are expected to wear the club tie!

The St. Barnabas Curry Club in Cambridge combines religion with the appreciation of curry and is a men's group within the eponymous church there. They meet approximately fortnightly, on Wednesdays, to enjoy good curry and erudite conversation. They normally get both, but apparently sometimes have to make do with neither!

After coming second in a Canterbury cook-off competition, Customs & Excise officer Paul Sing Babra decided to pursue his culinary hobby by starting a **Canterbury Curry Club**, and running Hot N Spicy evenings in Canterbury where fans can tuck into the spicy delights prepared by Paul himself.

Many curry clubs, not too surprisingly, seem to be associated with drinking.

The Club (we wonder how long it took them to think that up!) started as a bit of fun but soon became a mission - a mission to visit and rate every curry house within walking distance of the Dirty Dick's pub on Bishopsgate (London), although later, the meeting place changed to the King's Stores. In January 2002, they decided to broaden the scope - they can now meet at any pub within the official City of London limits and walk to a curry house from there. Membership of the Club is restricted to those who work, or have worked, on the GRD project at a prestigious City institution.

Milton Keynes Curry Club

Their Mission - To drink beer, eat curry and try and persuade the many curry houses in the Milton Keynes area that they really are part of the Egon Ronay empire, and should therefore be eligible for a significant discount - or lots of free beer.

Curry Club of Petersfield

The founder members

Johnny Walker: Fabled Rugby player and coach at Petersfield RFC and then in Spain, Johnny is now rumoured to be Chief Reporter of the Barrow-in-Furness Post.

Tim Anderson: Now living and working in France where he has a roofing business. Turned up for the meeting on 11th September 2002. When at home, his nearest curry house is in Poitiers.

Manor Park Curry Club - Great Malvern

Rules of the Curry Club

1) THE PRIME DIRECTIVE:

SPOUSE SHALL NOT ARGUE WITH SPOUSE

1b) Do not disagree with the Chairman.

2) A kitty for the purchase of beer shall be organised.

3) The Chairman must not forget the rules.

4) Anybody who orders a bottle of wine shall be banned.

5) No lime to be drunk with lager.

6) The preamble is irrelevant.

7) Leaving anything uneaten on your plate is not allowed.

8) A floating Chairperson will be elected on the night.

9) Meetings are not to be single sex.

10) People must ask the permission of the Chairman before going to inspect the plumbing.

11) "Curry" to be interpreted loosely. (See rule 12)

12) No meals to be English.

164

Bath University Curry Appreciation Society
voted BEST NEW SOCIETY OF THE YEAR 2002.
Up until now, their chief 'service' has been providing social outings to eat
curry at discount prices. This year they are going to be diversifying and
holding curry cooking courses as well as a planned pilgrimage to their
Mecca of curry, Birmingham.

THE Henley Regatta 10 CURRY CHALLENGE
Self-explanatory for those who have visited the event, really - those
accepting the challenge, attempt to have curry for lunch AND supper on
each of the five days of the regatta. This may sound easy but participants
normally fail on two counts.

Firstly, even the most hardened Thames curry club member is so smashed
on one (or more) of the days that they fail to make it to the curry house or,
worse still, fall asleep in their jalfrezi, thus failing for not eating.

The challenge is to have curry for lunch and dinner on each of the five days of the regatta.

Secondly, since the curry houses are all in town, they get too smashed to
walk that far, so resort to lunch in Remenham or the seafood and
champagne bar.

These and many more curry clubs exist all over Britain but the most
famous is **The Curry Club,** created by Pat Chapman and run by Pat and
his wife, Dominique.

Pat Chapman developed a passion for spicy food, which he virtually
inherited, at an early age. His family had lived in India for five generations,

Pat & Dominque Chapman deisplay their skills

and as a child, Pat regularly sampled his granny's curries, and was even fortunate enough to have visited the very few Indian restaurants in London at that time.

He became Marketing Manager with Lesney Products and was continually experimenting with Indian cooking, striving to recreate the curries remembered from his childhood. It was from this that The Curry Club was born.

Started in 1982 as a part-time venture, it grew rapidly and membership reached 15,000. Over the years Pat and Dominique have staged hundreds of curry nights around the country. Pat is a popular guest cook at food shows, on TV, takes groups of travellers on culinary tours to India, and his Curry Club residential weekend courses are renowned.

166

His many books have sold over one million copies, and titles include *The Curry Club Indian Restaurant Cookbook (Piatkus), Sainsbury's Curries, Balti Curry Cookbook, 250 Hot and Spicy Dishes from Around the World, Curry Club 100 Favourite Tandoori Recipes and Bangladeshi Restaurant Curries* - all published by Piatkus. His *Thai Restaurant Cookbook* and *Taste of the Raj* were both published by Hodder & Stoughton, and his more recent books were *The Curry Bible, The Vegetable Curry Bible* and *The Balti Bible.*

Beer Wars

A comment on curry houses would not be complete without mention of that necessary precursor to many curry meals - beer. Beer has been associated with curry in Britain as long as anyone can remember but there is no natural physical association, as neither beer nor lager will cool that chilli burn down.

Although the Prince of Denmark was responsible for the famous curry-lager marriage, the drink itself had reached our shores some years before.

Beer, or more precisely, lager, first became associated with curry at the famous Veeraswamy in 1927, soon after it opened. The Prince, soon to be King, of Denmark was in London visiting his sister, the Queen of England, and decided to dine at this new phenomenon that had arisen out of the grandeur of the Great Empire Exhibition. As always, he took his favourite brew with him, little knowing he was creating a precedent that would still be followed 75 years later.

167

Thus Carlsberg, brewed using the original yeast Saccharomyces Carlsbergensis, which had been discovered in 1847 by Captain J.C. Jacobsen, became the first beer to become identified with curry and most curry houses offered cold Carlsberg to their customers for over 50 years without any real argument from competitors. Carlsberg, Denmark's first lager beer, was launched on November 10th 1847 by J.C.Jacobsen in Valby, a small town on a hill overlooking Copenhagen, and it was named after his son Carl and 'berg', which when translated means 'on a hill'. The premium Export 5% lager is the brand best remembered in curry houses. However, as it was seemingly available in few other places in Britain where strong lagers were rare, this would come as only a mild surprise. Several of our dining companions over the years have also remarked that, at one time, Indian restaurants seemed to be the only draft outlets that could manage to serve it cold!

Although the Prince of Denmark was responsible for the famous curry-lager marriage, the drink itself had reached our shores some years before. Carlsberg was first brought to British shores by Danish sea captains, who shared their own personal supplies with friends and locals. Such was the popularity of the brand, that from 1868 supplies were regularly imported to the Edinburgh port of Leith.

168

WORKING MANS TOBACCONIST

SMOKE

GOODBODY'S RELIABLE

TOBACCOS

WESTALL'S

T. STORES

ESTD. 1849

T.WESTALL'S
DURABLE
BOOTS & SHOES
AT LOW
PRICES.

FOR ALL PURPOSES AND

IN EVERY STYLE & FITTING.

H. Naylor Covell's

SUPERIOR

TOBACCO & CIGARS

133   133

TANDOORI KNIGHTS
RESTAURANT & TAKE AWAY

KAOLA

1970 saw Denmark's two most important breweries, Carlsberg and Tuborg merge to form United Breweries Ltd, the group which then became Carlsberg A'S. In 1974 Carlsberg's UK operations were consolidated with the creation of the Carlsberg Brewery in Northampton. Not only does this now provide all the Carlsberg needs for the UK, but it has also become a showcase for modern brewing techniques and technology. In 1992 Carlsberg UK merged with the brewing division of Allied Lyons, Allied

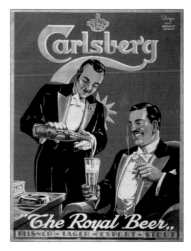

Breweries, to become Carlsberg Tetley. This now meant Carlsberg was sold in Allied's pubs. Since 1998 Carlsberg A'S has taken 100% ownership of Carlsberg-Tetley and more recently the company in UK has reverted to Carlsberg UK. Available in over 140 countries, Carlsberg is one of the most widely sold beers in the world.

Kingfisher was first imported into the UK in 1982, where it rapidly gained a foothold.

Carlsberg's prominence in Indian restaurants seemed assured until *Kingfisher* was first imported into the U.K. in 1982, where it rapidly gained a foothold in the fast expanding Indian restaurant market. The brand is owned by the multi-divisional conglomerate, UB Group of India, which operates in over 20 countries across Europe, North America, the Caribbean, the Middle East and Far East. It is the No. 1 selling lager in India with the lion's share

of the total massive Indian beer market.

Within three years, demand for the brand was so great that production had to be switched to England in order to keep up. Britain's oldest brewers, Shepherd Neame of Spitfire and other heady brews, were approached and agreed to brew Kingfisher under licence to the original Indian specification, at their brewery in Faversham, Kent. Today the U.K. operation is the supply centre for the brand's export to the U.S.A., Canada and 17 Continental European markets.

In the UK market, Kingfisher is claimed to be the leading Indian lager, particularly in draft sales, in the Indian restaurant sector, being sold in more than 6,500 of the 7,000 licensed outlets. The brand is also available in both large and small bottle sizes,

and is scoring increasing success in the U.K. take-home beer market, having gained listings at most of the major supermarket chains.

Kingfisher's latest product is Kingfisher Water which

India's Premium Lager

Kingfisher's award winning flavour and consistent excellence of quality has made Kingfisher the best selling Indian Lager in the world today.

GOLD AWARD WINNER
CLASS 2
INTERNATIONAL DRAUGHT
LAGER COMPETITION

THE BREWING INDUSTRY
INTERNATIONAL AWARDS
2002
BURTON UPON TRENT. U.K.

KINGFISHER
PREMIUM
Lager Beer

Most Thrilling Chilled!

KINGFISHER
PREMIUM LAGER BEER
India's Premium Lager

Brewing at UB, the home of Kingfisher, in days gone by

U.K.-brewed Kingfisher was awarded a Gold Medal in the pale lager class at the 1997 Chicago World Beer Championships to add to two consecutive Best Lager Awards in Sweden in 1994 & 1995. It also scooped the coveted Gold Medal, class 2 (ABV range of 4.6%-6.9%) in the International Draught Lager competition at The Brewing Industry International Awards 2002.

First brewed in 1857, Kingfisher is today the World's best selling Indian lager brand.

It was Britons flocking to Indian restaurants and gulping down his lager helped earn Karan Bilimoria of *Cobra Beer* the coveted "Asian of the Year Award for 2002" and many other prestigious awards.

Then a chance introduction with a brewer from Bangalore laid the foundation for a fresh business opportunity.

Born in Hyderabad, Karan Bilimoria is a son of Lt. General F.N. Bilimoria, PVSM, and ADC. Karan set off for England when he was 19. Initially, his education background was not well regarded when he applied to

175

join The Institute of Chartered Accountants in England and Wales (ICAEW), and he had to complete an accounting foundation course at the London Guildhall University in order to become eligible for registration as a student. He joined Ernst and Young as a trainee and in 1986 he qualified as a chartered accountant with the ICAEW. Later, he went to the Sidney Sussex College, Cambridge University to study law. It was during this period that Karan took up polo, and rose to captain Cambridge University's Blues polo team.

This hobby proved to be his launch pad into the business world, fuelling his first venture as a polo stick importer for clients such as Lillywhites and Harrods. Then , a chance introduction with a brewer from Bangalore, (who supplied to the Indian army), laid the foundation for a fresh business opportunity - selling Indian beer in England. In 1989 he started to import lager from the Bangalore brewery, christened it 'Cobra beer', and started marketing it to the Indian restaurants and grocers of Britain. In June 1997, beset by supply problems, he arranged for his beer to be brewed at the Charles Wells Brewery in Bedford, UK. Nowadays, a sizeable percentage of Indian restaurants stock Cobra beer, and it is available in 330 ml and 660 ml bottles, as well as on draft. Cobra then turned to other outlets; pubs, bars, nightclubs, supermarkets, world markets and off licence chains and, with a weather eye to changing trends, also introduced wines to the product line. Christened General Bilimoria wines after Karan's father, these were aimed to complement Indian food, alongside Cobra beer. Cobra beer, too, has won its share of plaudits. They have won a gold award from the Monde Selection, Brussels for four years running since 2001.

The Far East Beer Company was originally founded in 1993 to introduce speciality beers from the Indian sub-continent to the U.K., to complement the growing interest in Indian cuisine.

Their first beer brand was Lal Toofan, (Red Storm), which was brewed in the U.K. with the agreement of Shaw Wallace, one of the biggest brewers and distillers in India. Lal Toofan became popular on draught in Indian restaurants throughout the U.K., particularly in Scotland, and the Midlands.

In 1997 they launched Bangla in 660 ml bottles specially brewed at a higher strength of 5.5% ABV to complement stronger food with stronger flavours by brewmaster David Taylor. Bangla, in its distinctive, curved, bottle, has a growing following in London and the South East.

The Far East Beer Company is a small, enthusiastic team headed by Tosh Lakhani who took over from S. Walawalkar (who still acts in a support capacity) as managing director, both having worked at Kingfisher in earlier years. It is now part of Refresh UK plc, a new speciality drinks business which owns several other top brands.

UCB stands for *"Ultimate Curry Beer"* It is brewed by Banks's Brewery, which is situated in Wolverhampton, home to some of the best Indian restaurants, and which might explain the thinking behind the brewing of this beer. They also produce an excellent draught mild - although it's not called a mild anymore. It's no longer a fashionable term for some reason. Other dedicated 'curry' beers are *Ambari, Sunny Beaches, Bombay Pilsner, Bombay Export, Kohinoor, Gurkha, Adi Adi, Murree, Tikka Beer, Black Fort* and probably a few others that we have missed. Such is the publicity for Indian beers that many commentators miss the fact that many curry fans opt for ordinary bitter, particularly in North of England. In a recent survey, 22% of the regular curry-eating respondents went for Kingfisher, 21% for Cobra and 10% for Carlsberg but 10% also went for 'other' beers. Interestingly in the same survey 11% chose red wine as their drink of choice with a curry and 10% white.

CRITICS

A restaurant sector that turns over some £1.7 billion a year would seem to merit a great deal of media coverage, whether good or bad. Not a bit of it. There are merely a handful of 'experts' in journalism focusing on the Indian food and drink sector and the level of knowledge of those who do comment could often be improved upon.

Despite boasting Michelin-starred restaurants and a growing number of others that happily compete with the very best other cuisines have to offer, Indian food, or curry as we know it, is still given very much a secondary status in the world of the

Gordon Ramsay hands over yet another award to Rajesh Suri & Alfred Prasad of Tamarind, the only Michelin starred Indian restaurant at the time of writing.

restaurant critic. The trouble is that most have studied the classic French schools of cuisine, which do not, unfortunately, include the nuances of spicing needed for Indian cooking. Local newspapers will usually send along the office curry fan to cover new openings, especially as this will often mean a paid advertisement for their boss. At national level we have guides such as AA, Michelin, and Good Food, who pay lip service to Indian restaurants without giving many of them the recognition they deserve. The rare exceptions are Pat Chapman's *Good Curry*

Guide and our own *Real Curry Restaurant Guide*, now published on the internet at menu2menu.com.

Most national dailies also have an army of critics who cover Indian restaurants from time to time, showing varying levels of knowledge and understanding. Unfortunately their comments can have a very serious effect (sometimes beneficial, it must be said) on the restaurants on which they focus their attention.

Note the smart London Indian restaurant which was told, (in print), that their standards were so bad that it would be better if they closed down!; or another that was castigated because its owner was said to be too taciturn; or yet another that was torn to shreds in print, (based on a complimentary press preview), on the very day it was due to open its doors to a waiting culinary world. Many an Indian restaurateur has found himself scratching his head after his review wondering just what he did wrong.

Most of the best-known critics are based in London, so the restaurants there are usually the focus of their critiques - famous names such as Fay Maschler of the Evening Standard, Charles Campion of ES and The Times, Matthew Fort of The Guardian, Matthew Norman of Sunday Telegraph, Nicholas Lander of FT, Jay Rayner of The Observer, AA Gill of The Times, not to forget the irrepressible Michael Winner, who once found fault with almost everything on his first visit to, what is now, one of the top Indian restaurants in Britain. On the other side of the coin however, restaurants such as Chutney Mary, Zaika and Chowki in London have benefited hugely from positive reviews so it does seem to be a bit of a lottery.

Fortunately fans of Indian food are a very self-opinionated lot, so whilst a bad review can hurt both pocket and ego for a while, the customer will make the final decision, often based of a friend's or relative's recommendation - which is just the way it should be.

Curry Awards

Curry is taken seriously enough for there to be a whole plethora of 'awards' that one could scarcely imagine appearing in Italian or French cuisine. These usually take the shape of elaborate certificates stuck on the front window and, with few exceptions, are completely worthless as an indicator of the excellence or otherwise of the restaurants they claim to promote.

These are the so-called 'wallpaper awards', appropriately named because some restaurants have enough of them to wallpaper a wall. Trading Standards Officers have tried to stem the flow of these awards for many years but convictions are very hard to come by and both the givers of the awards and the receivers, the restaurants who hand over the money for them, seem to be very happy with the arrangement. Fraud, therefore, does not come into the picture - unless one takes into account the fact that the 'certificated' claims mislead the public .

There have been at least 20 organisations pushing 'wallpaper' awards over recent years, ranging from the waiter who travelled around with certificates in the back of his car in his spare time between shifts, to much more elaborate organisations claiming all sorts of quasi-official support.

Trading Standards has tried to stem the flow of these wallpaper awards for many years but convictions are very hard to come by.

Upon contact, the organisation will advise the restaurateur the cost of certification and what he will get for it. A few perfunctory questions are asked on an enquiry form (sometimes) and then, based on this worthless information (or none at all), the restaurant is awarded a four or five star award or even a 'Masters' certificate - the more elaborate the better. The chef of even the most modest establishment can be awarded a Master chef award without the certificate supplier ever having tasted his food! Certificates cost from £30 to over £150. There was one incident where one piece of paper cost over £750, including a supposed directory entry, which never appeared (and a lot of restaurants fell for it) with a fee having also been charged for extra copies. These awards entail no inspection visits, no industry knowledge by the certificators, and they are completely worthless. Strangely enough, many restaurateurs know they are worthless but still go for them!

This leads us neatly on to the *bona fide* awards from the major guides: *Michelin, AA, Good Food* (the Which one - not the fake, which is continually being pursued for copyright infringement by the Consumers' Association); and the two industry specialists, *The Real Curry Restaurant Guide,* and the *Curry Club, Good Curry Guide.* Each of the latter makes awards in editions of their guides and The Real Curry Guide organises the annual 'Best in Britain Awards' (BIBA), attended by the great and good of the industry each year. All of these guide awards are very

Adi Modi of Bombay Brasserie receives a BIBA award from Baroness Flather

181

carefully researched, involving personal visits and considerable industry knowledge, and therefore are not easy to come by. The BIBAs also recognise the major players in the industry with awards such as Restaurant Personality of the Year, Industry Personality of the Year.

Chef's awards are also keenly sought after and there are three major competitions annually that Indian chefs can enter to gain a coveted title. The longest running of these is Tommy Miah's *International Indian Chef of the Year* with its final in Edinburgh each year. This was followed by the *National Curry Chef of the Year,* organised by the Chartered Institute of Environmental Health through the local councils. This event started as the 'Hot Stuff Chef of the Year' in Bradford. It was the CIEH competition that produced the first white winner in Simon Morris of Grafton Manor, whose victory even produced a banner outside one restaurant in Manchester that read, 'Oh no! Beaten by a white man!' There is also the sector *Bangladeshi Chef of the Year* title to go for and other smaller titles promoted by commercial sponsors.

Each competition is completely separate with very different rules and restrictions, and the only time they have overlapped was when Taj International Hotels sponsored the Taj Spicemaster title in 2001. In this competition, staged at the Authentic Food Show at the NEC, Birmingham, the winners of the various titles took on seeded chefs from the top levels of the industry. International Indian Chef of the Year Veena Verma, a food lecturer from Birmingham won, much to the surprise of the pundits and seeded chefs.

Curry Community

Although the appreciation of curry is at its greatest in Indian restaurants, (not forgetting Thai, Malaysian or West Indian), there is a considerable

body of people who are restricted to home cooking or buying from the
supermarket, and yet another grouping who simply cannot wait for closing
time, and who enjoy a curry at their local pub.

With such examples as *Pele's Balti Pub* in Coventry and Trevor Gulliver's
Pukkabar in Sydenham, it looked as if the 'curry pub' was set to become a
national phenomenon, and one brewing group even had plans to roll out
the concept throughout Britain. Somehow the process seemed to grind to
a halt, however, so the curry pub has remained an isolated, though, popular
occurrence, such as the heaving *Glassy Junction* pub in Southall, just outside
London.

The curry industry has
enough characters and
noteworthy things in it
to fill ten books or a
whole TV soap. People
like *Enam Ali* creator
of Le Raj Avion,
whose idea of inviting
customers to dine on
Indian food whilst
flying around London
won his restaurant,
actually based in
Epsom, Surrey, an

*K.K. & Gulu Anand of Brilliant in Southall have been at the
forefront of the industry for 30 years*

innovation award from the City of London.

When mentioning notables within the sector, we cannot ignore *Mohammed
Aslam* of the Aagrah Group who went from bus driver to successful
restaurant group owner to star chef; restaurateurs who built their
restaurants wherever they could including sites such as ex-public toilets,

183

Charity

Very little publicity is given to the considerable contribution the Indian food and restaurant sector makes to charity in Britain but in most communities you will find Indian restaurants raising money for the local hospital, a cancer unit or even to provide showers, clean water and other basic facilities in the less well-off areas of Bangladesh, India and Pakistan.

Usually the fundraising is based around a special evening of food and entertainment where the customers are can have fun and do a little good at the same time. Even manufacturers join in, as was demonstrated when Seamark, suppliers of much of the seafood for the industry, raised £8,150 for the charity CRP, run by Valerie Taylor OBE in Bangladesh, which cares for people with spinal injuries. Perhaps the best-known national effort is that sponsored by Kingfisher lager. Originally launched as National Curry Day, the event has now grown to become Kingfisher World Curry Week.

During the eight years the event has taken place to date, well over £170,000 has been raised for good causes, ranging from The Prince's Trust and Save The Children to the present recipients, Action Against Hunger. This annual event invites Indian restaurants all over the country to help raise money for charity around a programme of fun and cultural education, with each participating restaurant holding its own special evening on behalf of charity.

The Army Catering team were up for a world record for Kingfisher World Curry Week

Attractions range from Bhangra dancing and karaoke to belly dancers. In the first year of the new format a lovely old double-decker bus was driven around the country, from Glasgow to Birmingham, handing out samples of curry in return for donations to the charity. The roadshow ended up at Kempton Park

Racecourse where a team from the Army Catering Corps broke the world record for the number of people served with a full Indian meal, cooked from scratch during racing (653), and Honeytop Foods baked the world's largest naan at over seven feet long.
The following year the currybus was off to Wales and the Home Counties, ending up at Kempton Park Racecourse just outside London once again. This time some of the top Indian chefs in the country cooked for racegoers in return for donations. The latest focus for this event was a national competition to find who could

build the highest Poppadum Tower and with the poppadum theme in mind, a designer even created a dress made entirely of poppadums. There is even a Curry Capital of Britain competition, also sponsored by Kingfisher Lager, which pitches Britain's major cities with a large Asian population against each other in a fun competition. London West romped to victory in the first year of the competition but were ousted by a sterling effort from the Glasgow team in the following year which was repeated a year later. Eventually Bradford, which had been second for three consecutive years went one better and took the title in 2004. Once again the aim is to raise money for charity.

Brian Dozey of Kingfisher hand the Curry Capital cup to Mayor Ken Livingstone

When it comes to charity, the Indian restaurateurs are amazing.
Restaurants such as *Juboraj* in Cardiff, *Britannia Spice* in Edinburgh, *Le Raj* in Epsom, *Kiplings* in Bradford, *Harlequin Group* in Glasgow, *Aagrah Group* in Yorkshire, and many more, offer an unparalleled example. Curry fans tend to be quite generous people if approached in the right way and this plus the religious imperative

Juboraj in Cardiff organise yet another fundraiser

of many restaurateurs to undertake charitable works ensures that 'we eat today so that others may eat tomorrow'.

185

churches, banks and public
buildings; *Daraz Aziz*, who opened
his first restaurant in
Northumberland in a railway
station and his next in a Pullman
Carriage; *Russ Kelly*, a man not
blessed with the best of health but
who travels the North of England
with his friend, visiting curry
houses and carefully rating them, at
his own expense and simply for his
own amusement; Abdul Latif, the
creator of 'curryhell' in Newcastle
who bought a defunct title and now

Daraz (Syed Nadir Aziz) of The Valley restaurant in Corbridge is one of the industry's colourful characters

has the right to be called Lord Harpole; *Kanchans* in Gants Hill, Essex,
which has a special ongoing donation to a local charity built into the
company's articles of memorandum as the owner's tribute to the memory
of his father; *Tommy Miah*, who even managed to get the Queen to write
the foreword to his book, Favourite Recipes of the Raj; and many, many
more.

*The curry industry has enough characters and noteworthy
things in it to fill ten books or a whole TV soap*

Curry is extremely popular for special occasions, ranging from garden
parties at Number 10 to the fantastic Asian weddings that take place
throughout the country. Companies such as Sanjay Anand's *Madhu's* in
Southall have grown to specialise in such events and watching them take

186

form is like watching a military manoeuvre being planned. From his purpose-built, steel clad kitchens in Southall he has catered for award ceremonies at the ultra smart Café Royal for over 300 in glittering brilliance without so much as batting an eyelid, and has coped with more than 1500 people attending a fantastic wedding reception at a top London hotel.

Madhu's Sanjay Anand

The industry even has its own publications apart from the many Asian community newspapers such as Menu Magazine, Tandoori, Roti(defunct), Asian Caterer(defunct), Spice Business, Masala and Khana Peena(defunct). Sadly, Khana Peena and Asian Caterer are no longer with us, and Roti flared for just one issue and died. Menu is a monthly publication, which covers all ethnic cuisines and, at the time of writing, is also the top internet publication (www.menu2menu.com & www.menumagazine.co.uk), and Spice Business is a quarterly specialist colour magazine which concentrates on the Bangladeshi sector. Tandoori has changed format completely since the days of co-founder and first editor, Iqbal Wahhab, when it was the top-rated monthly, having become more of a high-gloss coffee table quarterly.

Cooking the Books

It is not surprising that a cuisine as vast and complex as that of the Indian subcontinent has produced a multitude of cookery books. Most of these have been written by non-restaurant chefs, although the ones written by

187

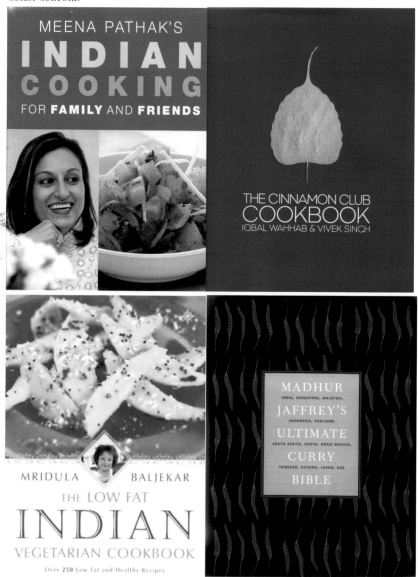

Cookery books from Meena Pathak of Pataks, Iqbal Wahhab with Chef Vivek Singh of Cinnamon Club, plus offerings from prolific writers Mridula Baljekar and Madhur Jaffrey

Cyrus Todiwala of Café Spice Namaste, Udit Sarkhel, then of Bombay Brasserie, now of Sarkhel's, Atul Kochhar of Benares and Das Sreedharan of the Rasa group, have probably been some of the best and most informative.

Most prolific of the non-restaurant chef writers is Pat Chapman of the Curry Club whose efforts total around thirty titles. Next on the ladder is Madhur Jaffrey, the Indian actress whose BBC Indian Cookery started it all, and who still has a huge following. With over a dozen titles we then have Mridula Baljekar, now owner of Spice Route in Windsor, and she has had enjoyed great success with her low fat recipes. Others include Simon Morris, Tommy Miah, Lali Nayar, Geeta Samtani, Sri Owen, and, more recently the top TV chef in India, Sanjeev Kapoor, as well as many others. Probably the most glossy of these works have come from two pillars of the industry.

Atul Kochhar of Benares

The first of these was one-time Taj International Hotel director, and now director of Masala World Restaurants, which includes Chutney Mary and Veeraswamy, Camellia Panjabi. Her book, *'50 Great Curries of India'*, was first

Writer & restaurateur Mridula Baljekar

published in 1994 by Kyle Cathie Ltd, to much critical acclaim. It is a very well worked and beautifully illustrated book and, for once, endeavours to explain the ethos behind Indian cuisine. The other is a volume produced by Sir Gulam Noon, the Chairman of the hugely successful Noon Food Products, which supplies chilled Indian foods under major supermarket brand names. Entitled, *'The Noon book of authentic Indian cookery'* and published by Harper Collins in 2001, its success was guaranteed when the words 'Foreword by Delia Smith' were printed on the front cover. Introduction and blessings from Sir George Bull, Chairman of J. Sainsbury Plc and David Felwick, Managing Director of Waitrose certainly didn't hurt either. Latest offering to become a must buy is The Cinnamon Club Cookbook by Iqbal Wahhab and top Chef Vivek Singh.

If you can stand the heat

The Indian cuisine industry is very different nowadays from those chaotic days of the sixties and seventies that saw much of the sector's initial growth. The restaurant was always the man's domain and whilst that is still mostly the case, there are women who are breaking the mould in the kitchen, front of house and ownership.

Ladies such as *Sherin Alexander Mody*, director of the Blue Elephant Group, which owns La Porte des Indes in London; *Mridula Baljekar*, who has confounded initial doubts about her ability to transfer her ideas from cookery books to restaurant with her highly acclaimed Spice Route in Windsor; *Pervin Todiwala*, whose impeccable front-of-house manner keeps the boardroom financiers in line at the Café Spice Namaste in the City;

Sisters *Camellia and Namita Panjabi*, who have long been ground-breakers for the sector with Chutney Mary, Masala Zone and their latest offering Amaya; *Perween Warsi*, who turned a small kitchen industry into a multi-million pound company; *Meena Pathak*, more than just the pretty face fronting the family business she and husband Kirit built up; *Nighat Awan*, owner of the Shere Khan restaurant group in Manchester and the sauces and pastes company of the same name; all are women who have come to the fore within an industry which once would have frowned at their mere involvement, let alone their leadership.

The restaurant was always a man's domain and while that is still often the case, there are many women who are breaking the mould.

Training for the industry is changing, too. In the past, budding chefs would have probably had to start their career as a porter, graduating to cutting up meat or onions, then on, perhaps, to the tandoor, and finally leaving to open their own restaurant (more often sooner than later, in many instances). More than a few simply did one stint in the kitchen in any capacity, or even just as a waiter, spent a few shifts watching the money head into their employers' cash registers, and fancied their chances as a restaurant owner. Nowadays most Universities and Colleges run courses in Asian cuisine that result in officially recognised NVQ qualifications, which may not completely prepare them for the hectic nightmare of a restaurant kitchen in full flow, but at least gives a good basic grounding in cooking together with an awareness of health and hygiene requirements. Restaurateurs *Atique Choudhury* (Yum Yum, Thai), *Holland Kwok* (Good

Atique Choudhry commentates as Cyrus Todiwala demonstrates at The Asian & Oriental School of Catering

Earth, Chinese) and *Cyrus Todiwala MBE* (Café Spice Namaste, Indian) got together to create The Asian and Oriental School of Catering in Hoxton Street, London N1, and this establishment is churning out hopeful chefs by the thousands throughout the ethnic Asian sector. The school has the support of the Government Office for London and the Savoy Educational Trust, amongst other partners. The possibilities are open to people of all backgrounds and persuasions so, if you can stand the heat, get into the kitchen.

Even so, most of the top Indian chefs in Britain still come from the management schools of *Taj International, Oberoi* or *Sheraton* Hotels with the sort of qualifications and background understanding and knowledge of all cuisines, as well as Indian, that is needed to reach the top.

192

In just under a century, curry, as it is known as in Britain, much to the understandable annoyance of the Indian cuisine purists, has gone from a cuisine only known by those with connections to India - either Raj or by birth, to something that is part of the fabric of British culture and society. A hybrid, it has a unique something that is very much part of India and the whole sub-continent - but also very British. A highly addictive - and successful - combination.

With almost 100 years' experience of eating curries (nearly 200 years if you go back to the very first Indian restaurant), the British consumer's knowledge of the food and its ingredients has grown considerably, especially in the past ten years.

Despite the increasing knowledge of curry lovers in Britain, there are still a few who remain curry virgins and still others who have lots of questions and reservations. To conclude this work we would like to address these questions and reservations. In doing so we continually refer to 'curry' as we have throughout these pages but recognise that, to the purist, every dish in Indian cuisine cannot be defined as a curry, even though it is the label that seems to be applied to all Indian cuisine in Britain.

In our defence, however, we would point out that despite the fact that the word is supposedly not used in India, many of the sub-continent's top chefs have been known to use it with regularity. Atul Kochhar, who was one of the first two Indian chefs in Britain to gain a Michelin star, says that, to his mind, his food served at his smart, restaurant *Benares* in Berkeley Square, London, though modern is "authentic Indian". Despite this, the English translation of many of the dishes in his new book, 'Indian Essence', contain the dreaded word - as in 'Almond lamb curry' and Black pepper chicken curry'.

Q : Is curry is fattening or bad for you?

A : Simple answer - no. It is a sweeping and frequently made generalisation though, possibly because of the most publicised aspect of curry culture - the lager that goes with and often before, the meal. The food itself has its good and bad aspects, just like any other world cuisine. If you choose Onion Bhaji (usually dripping with oil), Chicken Tikka Masala (often packed with double cream) or a creamy Korma, ghee brushed Naan and finish up with syrupy Gulab Jamun then it will not be long before your clogged arteries are protesting loudly. When all is said and done, the basic ingredients are pretty much the same, whatever the nationality of the chef. Ultimately, it is what is done to them that turns foods from life sustainers to life shorteners.

Once upon a time most Indian chefs cooked with ghee (clarified butter) and you could always see a film of oil on top of the curry when it was put before you. Fewer and fewer chefs now use ghee at all, realising that full flavour can still be gained with vegetable oil or no oil at all. Try the drier

dishes such as Spiced Lamb Chops, Chicken Tikka, Biryani or subtly spiced, dry-fry vegetable creations for healthy dishes and wonderful tastes, plus the considerable health benefits to be gained from the herbs and spices used.

Q: What do those Indian Restaurant names mean?

A: *Indus* - a major river; *Banaras (Benares)* - a sacred city; *Ashoka* - Mauryan ruler 269-232 BC; *Diwan* - Ministry of Revenue in Mughal Empire; *Diwan-I-Khas* - Private Audience Chamber; *Sonargaon* - golden village; *Kushan* - dynasty ending 240 AD; *Kohinoor* famous and fabulous Indian diamond; *Hawa Mahal* - Palace of Winds; *Shish Mahal* - Palace of Mirrors; *Anjanti* - famous town and relic site; *Rajput (Rajpoot)* - King's son/warrior prince; *Nawab* - viceroy/governor; *Lal Qila* - Red Fort; *Moti* - Pearl; *Mumtaz Mahal* - Excellent of the Palace; *Diwan-i-Am* - Hall of public audience; *Jaipur* - city near Agra; *Simla* - a hill station which became a summer camp resort for the British Raj; *Sirdas* - noble; *Shah Jahan* The name of a Mughal Emperor; *Azad* - free; *Bharat* - India; *Devi* - Mother Goddess; *Raja* - King; *Raj* - royal/ruler; *Maharajah* - very important king; *Maharani* - very important queen; *Mumbai* - Bombay; *Durbar* - court.

Above: Benares in London's Mayfair - named after the sacred city.
Below: Rajdoot in Birmingham - named after the legendary warrior princes.

Perhaps one of the most romantic names used in the industry is that of *Anarkali,* one of the central characters in a legend that has grown up around actual historical figures. She was, supposedly, a stunningly beautiful dancing girl at the court of Akbar the Great, the 16th century Moghul Ruler. Prince Salim, (1569-1627, son of Akbar and a Hindu Rajput princess from Amber), had already angered his father by pronouncing himself king during the ruler's absence from the court at Agra. Akbar was able to wrestle the throne back and, amazingly for the times, Salim was allowed to live on to enjoy even further friction with his father. This was to come in the form of Salim's amorous infatuation with an ordinary dancing girl.

Salim fell deeply in love with a dancer, named Pomegranate Blossom by Akbar himself.

 Nadira Begum was a dancing girl at the Royal Court and a favourite of the Emperor, and had been re-named Anarkali, (Pomegranate Blossom), by Akbar himself. Deeply in love, Salim was ready to make her his queen. This union, not surprisingly, was unacceptable to Akbar. One version of the legend ends with the girl being abducted by Royal agents and deported to a far-off land. A far darker ending to the tale, however, is that in 1599 the Emperor ordered that this jewel of the court be walled up, alive. Salim finally came to power and re-named himself Jahangir, (The World Conqueror) and even got to marry a dancing girl - even though she wasn't his first choice. Today, the tomb of Anarkali is a tourist attraction in Lahore, situated in a corner of the Civil Secretariat of Punjab.
Many Indian restaurants are named after cities such Bombay, or Agra, sometimes for regions as in Himalaya, or landmarks as in Taj Mahal, Everest, Ganges or Khyber. There was a trend for a while of naming new restaurants after famous films, as in Jewel in the Crown and Passage To India. In recent times, however, there has been a tendency to use spice names as in Elaichi - cardamom or Zafran - saffron.

199

Q :Does Chicken Tikka Masala have to be red to be authentic?

A :Simple answer - no.
Firstly, as a British Indian
creation with no
acknowledged official
recipe, it could really be
any colour you want it to
be. The great British
public, however, seems to
think it should be red,
with shades varying from a
gentle maroon to a bright,
almost radioactive colour.
Strangely enough this has
even extended to the
chicken tikka itself, which
many people will only eat

and enjoy if it is red. Sorry to disappoint you but there is no reason for
chicken tikka to be red, unless colouring is used. We think that it certainly
tastes best with a natural, slightly golden hue. Our youngest daughter, for
example, won't touch chicken tikka if it is bright red, even going as far as
to state that the colour makes it 'taste funny'. There is more reason for the
Masala (sauce) part to be red, as tomatoes are used in most of the recipes
for the dish, but this does not excuse the lurid brightness of some of the
finished products, both in the restaurant and purchased from
supermarkets. If a dish is unnaturally bright in colour then food colourings
(those dangerous 'E' numbers) have been used and that is not only
unnecessary but illegal, depending on the amount used.

Q: **Is it true that chilli eating is an acquired habit?**

A: This time - yes.

It is the 'chilli burn' that puts many people off Indian food initially, which is unfortunate, as the excellence of Indian food bears no relation to the chilli heat of the dish. Restaurants usually start people off with a creamy

korma, which though incorrectly labelled, has become the dish of choice for the 'curry virgin' in Britain. Moving on to the sampling of companion's dishes or side dishes will lead on to selections with a stronger taste and, over the years, a

stronger and stronger chilli taste is required to achieve the same pleasurable sensation in the brain that keeps you coming back for more (see Chapter 3). Some fans even have to ask for a plate of small green chillies to be put on the table to eat during the meal, such has their resistance grown.

Q: **Should hot dishes leave you with a burning sensation?**

A: Yes and no.

If the spices are cooked correctly, no chilli burn should go further than the mouth and should never reach the throat or stomach, as this indicates incorrectly cooked spices. There is no point in swallowing gallons of lager or water to put the burn out, should it happen, but rather any milk-based product, such as the Indian yoghurt drink, lassi. The balance of spices lies at the heart of good Indian cuisine and the right spicing for each dish can take a lifetime of experience.

Q :Do visits to Indian restaurants usually end up in the bathroom?

A: No - and they certainly shouldn't.

Much of the 'toilet' humour surrounding curry suggests that an uncomfortable visit to the bathroom next day is part and parcel of enjoying a night out at an 'Indian'. Properly cooked Indian food will never have an adverse effect of this nature, no matter how chilli-hot the dish. Again, it is that expression 'properly cooked' that is the key to this often-encountered problem. Some curry houses operate on such low margins that quick turnarounds are needed. Couple this with the fact than many customers do not want to wait long for their food, and it is not surprising that spices are often added at the last minute and are not properly cooked. This irritates the digestive system and makes you a prime candidate for the smallest room. Another and more probable reason is poor storage of cooked rice which, when kept hanging around too long, (possibly as a takeaway), and not being hot all the way through, is an ideal breeding ground for a nasty little bug called Bacillus Cereus. This has a very short incubation period and the reaction can, indeed, be serious! It is, however, often not the food at all that causes the effect but the seven pints of lager that went with it!

Q: Is it true that wine does not go with spicy food?

A: Very definitely - no.

The traditional wine menu of the curry house of twenty years ago usually listed such 'classics' as Blue Nun, Black Tower, Piesporter Michelsberg and any old bin end the local wine merchant could offload onto an unsuspecting teetotal restaurateur. Quality didn't really matter - because wine experts said that wine didn't go with spicy food. Then, some Indian

11.5% vol   75cl

L0001

Rája Rosé™

semi-sparkling
medium dry wine

Produced and bottled by RE 4323–GE, Girona, Spain
for Wine for Spice Ltd, London W2 2YQ, UK

Wine of Spain

203

restaurants moved very much up-market and spicing became more subtle. Suddenly the food was no longer merely fodder to go with pint after pint of your favourite brew. Top wine experts still tended to shy away from Indian cuisine with their treasured choices but a new breed of wine master was to emerge; experts who understood the food as well as wine and realised there was a whole new world out there, with specific wines which complemented spicy food to perfection. Though often not drinkers themselves, for religious reasons, the restaurateurs were quick to catch on and wine lists began to change rapidly, which, happily, introduced another dimension to the customer and a bigger spend-per-head to the restaurateur.

Q: Is it true that an Indian meal should start with poppadoms?

A: Unfortunately no.

The eating of poppadoms and chutnies at the beginning of the meal whilst waiting for your starter and sipping your lager is a British Indian restaurant habit, and one which can be very important to the restaurant in revenue terms. Poppadoms are usually 50-60p each despite costing a negligible amount to produce, so the sight of you wading through a stack of those giant crisps gladdens a restaurateur's heart. In traditional Bengali cuisine, for instance, poppadoms are served after the main course but fear not, we don't think this will catch on in Britain. The average British curry fan consumes one and a half poppadoms with each meal. One supplier alone in Chennai maintains he exports 2 million poppadoms a day to Britain's top supermarkets and restaurants.

Q: **Why don't those supermarket meals ever taste the same as restaurant ones?**

A: · This is a difficult one.

If you want your Indian meal to taste the same as in a restaurant the answer is simple - go to a restaurant. Restaurants batch-cook in most instances and have access to a far wider range of herbs, spices and other products than you are likely to be able to find for your home cooking or get in a ready meal. Also Indian cuisine is very anarchic and many restaurant chefs operate by experience and instinct and couldn't tell you the exact measurements (and wouldn't if they could!). Companies that manufacture supermarket chilled and frozen products also batch-cook and have improved tremendously over the years. Top suppliers such as Noon, Patak and S&A have armies of highly qualified chefs in their research kitchens, all dedicated to improving and refining products all the time, but the main problem lies in the nature of the product. Firstly, they have to have an economic shelf life - meaning that they contain varying levels of preservative, which

Some products, such as this curry from Noon in collaboration with top London restaurant Quilon, come closer than others.

205

can often give a metallic aftertaste. Secondly, spices deteriorate and change at different rates, so the taste balance can change, depending on length of time stored. On the plus side, the range offered by supermarkets is now huge, and gives the more timid curry fan the opportunity to try out hitherto unknown regional dishes before going for it in a big way in a restaurant.

Q: So where do we go from here?

A : No, the answer is not 'I'm off for a Chinese'.

Contrary to the odd newspaper article looking for sensation, there is no evidence the Indian sector is in decline. You just have to look around at some of the fantastic new Indian restaurants opening up week after week to see that the sector itself doesn't believe it. Of course there is no divine right for Indian restaurants to survive but, not only is it part of British culture now, but its members are some of the most naturally adaptable people in the entire restaurant community - and there is no reason to think they won't continue to adapt as market requirements change.

It is unlikely that there will be another 'fad' to give the industry a boost, along the lines of tandoori or balti. Others have been suggested, such as haandi, tawa and thali but these have not caught on as national labels and are likely to remain part of the greater panoply of attractions that make up Indian cuisine. Even if a new 'fad' were magically to appear, the Indian restaurant scene is not set up in the same way it was fifteen years ago. Now there is a clear distinction between the high street curry house and the more upmarket Indian restaurant focusing on regional cuisine. In between you have the curry houses that have recognised the need for change from the red-flocked wallpaper days and have invested in often elaborate and expensive refurbishments, without necessarily doing the same for their menu.

*Top quality Indian cuisine from Chef
Stephen Gomes of Café Naz, Cardiff*

The future of curry in Britain is, in a way, already here. No longer is it the cheap alternative; the 'so who cares about the quality' attitude on which it built its popularity is rapidly becoming outdated. Restaurants are finding themselves having to become more professional as rules and regulations tighten. Gone - or at least going - are the days when an owner can simply employ his extended family regardless of experience; days are numbered, too for cash-in-hand payments, no questions asked. The days are also gone when anybody could be drafted into the kitchen when needed - and who cares about health and hygiene anyway? Company books are having to be regularised, employment contracts considered, staff trained and so on, and all these put up the overheads. Curry houses also have increased competition to face from supermarkets and other cuisines, such as Thai and Mexican, both of which also have the 'chilli-kick' attraction.

So how can the Indian restaurant keep ahead of the competition? Two of the options are to improve the spend-per-head or turn the customers around quicker. If the former is chosen it means a more varied, better quality menu, which means good kitchen staff, and front of house staff that can communicate, as they are professional salesmen and women. If the latter, then the customer has to be made comfortable - but not too comfortable - and the service needs to be really snappy, with dishes designed to be consumed quickly. Ashoka Shak in Scotland and Masala Zone in London have already shown the way in this direction. Whatever the route, the curry industry is on the move, with the accent swinging to quality rather than quantity.

It is probable that the total number of Indian restaurants in Britain will go no higher than the 9,000 plus it is at present, possibly slacking off a little, as sons and daughters decline to follow the example of their fathers in working long, unsociable hours. We will probably see greater emphasis on regional cuisine; more movement into the fast food market - after all, even

Quality & value at Masala Zone

MacDonalds recognised the attraction and tried to produce their own rather sad version of Indian food; more top class restaurants with top class Indian chefs battling for Michelin stars; more than just lip-service paid to the health aspect of Indian dishes; more refurbishments to provide a light, bright dining atmosphere.

With all these inevitable changes, will the basic curry house we all know, love and lampoon still be around? Of course it will. It's an institution and, as long as there is a bunch of students who want to go out for a curry on a Friday night, or a rugby team that wants to go 'Indian' for their annual bash, the good old-fashioned curry house will be there to provide its unique, value-for-money service.

Curry, whether from the restaurant, as a takeaway, cooked at home or from the supermarket, is part of the rich fabric of British culture of today - and long may it remain so.

GLOSSARY

Aam Mango
Aam chur Mango powder
Achar Pickle
Adrak Ginger
Ajwain Lovage
Akroot Walnuts
Aloo Potato
Aloobukara Plum
Amjeer Figs
Ananas Pineapple
Anar Pomegranate
Atta Chapati flour
Badam Almond
Baingan Egg plant/brinjal
Besan Gram flour
Bindi Okra/Ladie fingers
Bhajia Fried
Bombay Duck Dried fish
Chawal Saffron rice
Dahi Yoghurt
Dalchini Cinnamon
Dhania Coriander leaves
Doodhi Bottle gourd
Ekuri Spicy scrambled eggs
Elaichi Cardamon

Gajar Carrot
Garam Masala Spice mix
Ghee Clarified butter
Gobi Cauliflower
Gosht Meat
Gur Jaggery
Handi Eathernware cooking pot
Mari Mirchi Green hot chilli
Hing Asafoetida
Imli Tamarind
Jal frezi Sautee or stir fry
Jeera Cumin
Jhinga Prawn
Kalimirchi Peppercorns
Kaju Cashew nut
Kalongi Nigella
Karahi Two handled cooking pan
Karela Bitter gourd
Kari Pata Curry leaves
Kesar or Zafron Saffron
Kheer Milk pudding
Khuskhus Poppy seeds
Lal Mirchi Red chilli pepper
Lasun Garlic
Lavang Cloves

Malai Cream
Methi Fenugreek seeds
Moong Dal Green lentil
Palak Sinach
Paneer Cheese
Puri Deep fried unleavened bread
Sabzi Vegetables
Samosa Stuffed pastry
Saunf Fennel
Seviyan Vermicelli
Shahi Royal

Shashlick Skewered pieces of meat
Srikhand Saffron yoghurt
Tarla Dal Spiced lentil puree
Tawa Heavy steel shallow frying pan
Til Sesame seeds

Tinda Gentleman's Toes
Urad Dal Black lentils
Vindaloo Originally a Portuguese dish
words for wine & garlic (not potato)
Yakni Mutton

Sherin Alexander-Mody at La Porte des Indes in London

South Indian style at Quilon

BIBLIOGRAPHY

The authors would like to acknowledge the input from the following volumes and the many other avenues of research used to create this work.

Royal Recipes	Michele Brown	Pavilion
Legacy of the Indus	Samina Quraeshi	Weatherhill
Archaeology of the World	Courtlandt Canby	Chancellor
A Dash of Spice	Hawkins & Duff	Readers Digest
A History of Roman Britain	Peter Salway	Oxford University
Bengali Cooking	Chitrita Banerji	Serif
Bridge on British Beef	Tom Bridge	Piatkus
Chinese Cookery Encyclopedia	Kenneth Lo	Collins
The Complete Meze Table	Rosamund Man	Garnet
Indian Cookery	Mrs Balbir Singh	Mills & Boon
Traditional Greek Cooking	George Moudiotis	Garnet
The Food of Italy	Claudia Roden	Arrow
Traditional Spanish Cooking	Janet Mendel	Garnet
50 Great Curries of India	Camellia Panjabi	Kyle Cathie
Complete Mexican Cookbook	Lourdes Nichols	Piatkus
The Food Medicine Bible	Earl Mindell	Souvenir Press
Book of Fruit & Fruit Cookery	Paul Dinnage	Sidgwick & Jackson
The World Atlas of Food		Spring Books
In Search of the Trojan War	Michael Wood	BBC
Mythology	Richard Cavendish	W.H.Smith
World Prehistory	Grahame Clark	Cambridge Univ
Fabulous Feasts	Madelaine Pelner Cosman	George Braziller
The Food of Japan	Wendy Hutton	Periplus
Curries & Bugles	Jennifer Brennan	Viking
Savouring The Past	Barbara Ketcham Wheaton	
(The French Kitchen Table 1300-1789)		Chatto & Windus

The Oxford Companion to Food	Alan Davidson	Oxford U.
A History of India	Romila Thapar	Penguin
History of Hospitality	David Goymour	
Great Household in Medieval England	C.M. Woolgar	Yale University
Hobson-Jobson	Henry Yule & A.C.Burnell	Wordsworth
Harvest of the Cold Months	Elizabeth David	Michael Joseph
Beeton's Book of Household Management		Chancellor
Food (An Oxford Anthology)	Brigid Allen	Oxford U.
The Raj at Table	David Burton	Faber & Faber
The Roots & Tales of Bangladeshi Settlers	Yousuf Choudhury	
The Peopling of London	Nick Merriman	Museum of London
The Might that was Assyria	H.W.F.Saggs	Sidgwick & Jackson
On Food & Cooking	Harold McGee	Harper Collins
The Dawn of Civilization	Stuart Piggott	Thames & Hudson
National Restaurant Directory	Peter & Colleen Grove	Belgrove Publishing
London & Its People	John Richardson	Barrie & Jenkins
London a Social History	Roy Porter	Hamish Hamilton
Food in Antiquity	D. & P. Brothwell	Thames & Hudson
Savouring The East	David Burton	faber & faber
Food - The Gift of Osiris	Darby, Ghalioungui & Grivetti	
In Praise of the Potato	Lindsey Bareham	Penguin
Food	Clarissa Dickson Wright	Ebury Press
A Concise History of the Darjeeling District since 1835	E.C. Dozey	
Under the patronage of Rt Hon Baron Carmichael of Skirling G.C.I.E. K.C.M.G. first Governor of Bengal		
History of the World	W.N. Weech	Odhams
The Frank Muir Book	Frank Muir	Wm Heinemann Ltd
Myths & Legends - China & Japan	Donald A. Mackenzie	Gresham Publishing
The Travels of Dean Mahomet	Dean Mahomet	U. of California
Food Culture in India	Colleen Taylor Sen	Greenwood Publish.

INDEX

AA Guide	178, 181
Aagrah Group	57, 142
Aakash	142
Aberdeen Angus	81
Aethelred II	14
Ahad, Abdul	138-139
Ahmed, Iqbal	95
Ahmed, Manzoor	86
Ali, Amin	66, 70, 88, 100, 133, 136
Ali, Enam	70, 121, 138-139, 183
Ali, Mosrof	50
Ali, Rajiv	54
Ali, Rashid	52
Almedia, Francisco-de-	20
Anand, Gulu	183
Anand, K.K.	183
Anand, Sanjay	186-187
Ansari, Sultan Ahmed	52,88
Asda	98, 99, 122
Asian & Oriental School of Catering	192
Aslam, Mohammed	57, 143-144, 183
Aziz, Abdul	51
Aziz, Syed Nadir	186
Bacillus Cereus	202
Bahadur, Bir	46, 49, 52
Bahadur, Shomsor	49
Bahadur, Sordar	49
Baljekar, Mridula	9, 65, 91, S188-189, 190
Balti	61-65, 99, 118
Baltistan	62-63
Beefeater	78, 81
Bengal Clipper	157, 160
Berni Inns	78, 79, 81
Best In Britain Awards	181-182
Bhajwe, Raj	146-147, 158, 161
Bhatia, Navin,	134, 135
Bhatia, Vineet	131-132, 134
Bilimoria, Karan	175-176
Birmingham	94, 150
Biryani	93
Bokth, Malik	52
Bombay Brasserie	66-68, 100, 126-127, 136
Bombay Palace	134-135
Boulanger	38
Branson, Sir Richard	134, 162
Brick Lane	147-149
Brilliant, Southall	183
Butlin, Billy	72
Café Lazeez	93, 134-135
Café Naz	207
Café Spice Namaste	130, 190
Callaghan, James	79
Campion, Charles	88, 179
Capsiacin	101-103, 106
Carling Black Label	93
Carlsberg	54, 167-171
Cathay	71-72
Chapman, Pat	12, 65, 165-167, 189
Chappatti	117-118
Chaudhry, Atique	191-192
Chicken Tikka Masala	10, 24, 52, 84-90, 92,
	99-101, 116, 200
Chilli	10, 103-105, 107, 201, 208
Chop Suey	80
Chor Bizarre	55, 57, 70, 133
Chutney Mary	55-56, 100, 128-129, 179, 189
Cinnamon Club	69-70, 124-125, 130, 188
Cobra	54, 175-176
Columbus, Christopher	19
Cook, Robin	10
Crusades	15
Curry Club, The	165-167, 181
Curry Clubs	162-165
Davidson, Alan	12, 89
Daraz	184
David, Elizabeth	78
Dharan	52
Dom Alfanso d'Alberquerque	17, 20-21
Durbar	50-51
Dutch East India Company	36
Elizabeth I	19
Empire Exhibition	53, 76, 167
English East India Company	19, 32, 36, 42-43, 71
Escoffier, Georges Auguste	40-41
Far East Beer	176-177
Forme of Cury	17-18
Gama, Vasco da	17, 20-21
Garlic	109
Gaylord	56
George IV	31
George V	54
Gill, Charan	145-146
Ginger	14
Glasse, Hannah	24
Gofur, Abdul	50
Gomes, Stephen	207
Good Food Guide	80, 178, 181
Gupta, Niru	90
Haris, Iftekar	10
Harlequin Leisure	145
Harnal, Arun	126-127
Harriett, Ainsley	116
Hindostanee Coffee House	25, 28
Hobson-Jobson	22
India National Congress	32
Jaffrey, Madhur	25, 188-189
Jaffrey, Saeed	159
Jahangir	19
Jaipur	138-139
J. Lyons & Co	76-77
Juboraj	183
Kanchans, Gant's Hill	186
Kapoor, Sanjeev	118-119, 189
Karim, Abdul	28, 32
Kashmir	83
Kaul, Mahendra	56, 60, 133
Khalique, Sheik Abdul	88
Khattar, Rohit	60, 133
Kingfisher	54, 12-121, 171-173, 175, 184-185
Kingfisher World Curry Week	121, 184-185
Kochhar, Atul	131, 189, 196
Koh-I-Noor	42

214

Koon, Chung	71
Koon, John	72
Korma	92, 94, 196
Kutub, Ahmed	52
Kwok, Holland	191
La Porte des Indes	70, 133, 135
Lal, Kundan	56
Lal Toofan	54, 174-175
Lascars	39
Latif, Abdul	186
Lea & Perrin	25
Leicester	149-150
Le Raj	70, 121, 138-139, 183
McDonalds	78, 209
Mahmood Ali, A.H.	33
Mahomet, Dean	25, 28-31, 44
Malcolm, Stephana	24
Manchester	151-152
Markham, Gervase	22
Marks & Spencer	10, 122
Marot, Clement	38
Masala Zone	129, 208
Maschler, Fay	136, 179
Master, Ayub Ali	50
Mathrani, Ranjit	46, 56
Menu Magazine	187
Merchant, Ismail	68, 133
Miah, Afrose	52
Miah, Gofur	46
Miah, Israil	46, 50
Miah, Lal	52
Miah, Sanu	50
Miah, Tommy	144, 162, 182, 189
Michelin	6, 70-71, 134, 178, 181, 196, 209
Modi, Adi	66, 97, 126-127, 181
Mody, Mehernosh	135
Mody, Sherin Alexander	133, 135, 184-185
Mohammed, Reza	134
Moneer, Mohammed	91
Montagu, John, 4th Earl of Sandwich	41
Morris, Simon	117, 182, 189
Mumtaz	142
Naoriji, Dababhai	44
Noon Products	10, 205
Noon, Sir Gulam (G.K.)	89, 97-98, 190
Panjabi, Camellia	12, 68, 124-126, 189-191
Panjabi, Namita	46, 70, 126, 128, 191
Patak's	95, 186, 205
Pathak, Kirit	95
Pathak, Meena	95, 188
Pepys, Samuel	28
Prince of Denmark	54, 167
Polash	54, 88
Poppadoms	204
Prasad, Alfred	132, 178
Pulze, Claudio	130
Quilon	70, 126
Rajitsinhji	44-45
Rashim, Abdul	50
Razzah, Haji Abdul	54, 88
Real Curry Restaurant Guide	181
Red Fort, Soho	46, 70
Richard I	15-16
Richard II	17
Rosee, Pasqua	37-38
Roy, Amit	84
Safeway	99
Sainsbury	10, 98, 122
Salut ç Hind	45
Samtani, Geeta	99, 189
Sandys, Lord Marcus	25
Sarkhel, Udit	68, 126, 136-137, 159, 189
Sarkhel, Veronica	136
Sattar, Dr Abdul	161
Scoville Scale	107
Sepoy Mutiny	32
Shafi	45-48
Sharwoods	98
Shere Khan	99
Singh, Duleep	42
Singh, Kuldeep	135-136
Singh, Mrs Balbir	91
Singh, Vivek	125
Sondhi, Deepinder Singh	60
Soyer, Alexis	40
Sreedharan, Das	189
Sriram, A.V.	128
Star of India	66, 134
Sunderam, Vikram	126-127
Suri, Rajesh	6-7, 132, 178
Sylhet	10, 49, 51, 88
Taillevent (Guillaume Tirel)	17, 26
Tamarind	6-7, 70, 132, 178
Tandoor	54, 58-59
Tata, J.R.	68
Tesco	90, 122
Thakeray, William Makepeace	23
Thrakrar, Rashmi	96
Tilda	96
Todiwala, Cyrus	70, 130-131, 140-141, 189, 192
Todiwala, Pervin	131, 141, 190
Tristao, Nuno	17
Turmeric	112
Uddin, Nojir	52
Uddin, Dr Wali Tassar	144-145
Unani Tibb	109
Uncle Ben's	89
Vama, The Indian Room	70, 134, 137, 159, 162
Varma, Andy	70, 134, 137, 159, 162
Varma, Moni	96
Veeraswamy	46-49,54, 56-57, 76, 129, 167
Victoria	28, 42, 157
Vindaloo	18, 81, 92, 94, 116
Wahhab, Iqbal	70, 88, 124-125, 130, 187
Waitrose	10, 89, 98, 122
Warsi, Perween	99
William IV	31
William The Conqueror	14
Wimpy	78
WT Foods	98
Zaika	70, 130

215